Managing and developing new forms
of work organisation

Managing and developing new forms of work organisation

Second (revised) edition
Edited by George Kanawaty

Nitish De
Sven Flykt
George Kanawaty
Rolf Lindholm

Håkan Lundgren
Anders Malmberg
Jan-Peder Norstedt
Einar Thorsrud

SCHOOL OF
CALIFORNIA
PROFESSIONAL
PSYCHOLOGY
LOS ANGELES

Management Development Series No. 16

International Labour Office   Geneva

ISBN 92-2-102707-4

First published 1980
Second (revised) edition 1981
Second impression 1984

Printed in Switzerland

CONTENTS

FOREWORD

It is difficult to trace the beginning of interest
in new forms of work organisation. Several experiments
in this field may have been carried out at different
times by different enterprises around the world without
being clearly identified and without being recorded.
The work of the Tavistock Institute of Human Relations
in India in the fifties and the pioneering work in
Norway and Sweden in the early sixties, which spread to
many countries, had one thing in common. In designing
and modifying work, one needs to consider the technical
and the social issues together. Thus, improved methods
of work based on better planning and control or on the
redistribution of assignments and responsibilities have
to be reconciled with the social needs of the working
group in terms of factors such as the variety and the
degree of challenge the job offers, the opportunities
for learning and advancement and so on. The new forms
of organisation, therefore, represents an optimum result
between the technical demands of the job and the social
needs of the people performing it. Another important
feature of this approach is participation by the people
involved in designing their own work. This aspect has
been emphasised since the early days of experimentation,
particularly in the Scandinavian countries, and has given
rise to the "industrial democracy" concept often used in
Norway.

The growing interest in new forms of work organisation since the late sixties has been accompanied by an
explosion of the literature dealing with this area in
particular, and with the quality of working life in
general. The literature falls mainly into two groups.
First, a descriptive approach showing how a certain
experiment was carried out in a given working situation.
Second, a synopsis of various experiments, which concludes by extolling the merits of the new approach as a
cure for organisational ineptness.

Relatively little has been published, however, on
the course that needs to be followed in introducing the
change in various enterprises, and much less on the
implications of such a change for the various functions
of enterprise management.   For example, redesigning a
production system can trigger and sometimes be reinforced
by a corresponding change in the accounting system or in
personnel policy.   The purpose of this book is to fill
this gap.

The book is intended for managers, consultants,
trade unionists and others interested in the field.
It can assist them in identifying a priori the implications of developing new forms of work organisation.   It
also provides a guide on how to go about introducing the
change in the various domains of activities of an enterprise.

The first chapter, written by Einar Thorsrud, deals
with the organisational structure of the new forms of
work organisation, outlining the differences between it
and traditional organisations, and the new roles for
working group members, for supervisory staff and for
specialists that result from the organisational change.
Rolf Lindholm and Sven Flykt, in the second chapter, deal
with the design of production systems, including the
principles of grouping production equipment, those of
modifying transport, those of handling and stocking and
also the new approaches to production planning and control, quality control and maintenance operations.   The
third chapter, written by Anders Malmberg, is a refresh-
ing look at accounting and internal financial reporting
systems under new forms of work organisation.   It cites
two case studies where the new systems were successfully
introduced.   In the fourth chapter Nitish De examines
the implications for personnel management of new forms
of work organisation, particularly in the areas of
recruitment, selection, training, career development
and union relations.   He supports his views with cases
from Indian enterprises.   The fifth chapter, written by
Håkan Lundgren and Jan-Peder Norstedt, deals with
remuneration in relation to new forms of work organisation and provides an insight into prevailing trends in
this area.   Finally, George Kanawaty, in the sixth and
last chapter provides a guide to introducing new forms
of work organisation, shows how it can be applied in
different situations and cites several examples.

THE CHANGING STRUCTURE OF WORK ORGANISATION

1

Einar Thorsrud*

If we pass through a monotonous landscape we gradually stop expecting something new to appear along the
road.   After a while we may even overlook the variation
that exists.   If we have to walk a road through such a
landscape we may end up like sleepwalkers.   If we drive
a car we are in danger of running into a serious accident.

Work organisation in industrial societies developed
in the same direction for nearly a century.   Mechanisation, specialisation and standardisation were the main
principles used to change products and procedures.   Over
time this had its effects on people as well.   The same
patterns spread from the factory to the office and then
to the school and the hospital and so on.   The organisational landscape became monotonous and a lot of people
started to behave like sleepwalkers or like bored and
irritated passengers in motor cars.   Many of those at
the steering wheels of organisations stopped keeping
their eyes on the road.   Accidents occurred everywhere.
Only a few outsiders saw that the landscape had started
to shift in a fundamental way.

In retrospect we can see how it was possible for
this to happen.   Organisations are created by men, but
after a while it is the other way round.   Organisations
create men in their own image and according to their own
needs.   When this occurs the consequences can be serious.   A vicious circle can be created in one part of
society, and if this part has a powerful influence on
others the total effect can be disastrous.   Such a
development may have provided the background to the
uneasy feeling among people of the industrialised world
during the 1960s and 1970s.   This uneasy feeling had
been expressed by many authors like Orwell in <u>1984</u> and

---

* Einar Thorsrud is a Professor at the Work Research
Institute, Oslo.

Whyte in <u>Organization Man</u>.   There were other reasons
for anxiety.   There was the threat of nuclear war and
ecological crisis, but we should not underestimate the
psychological and political effects of the way in which
we organise work.

In retrospect we can see that we needed a number of
deviating cases of new forms of organisation before we
could grasp the basic nature of the old form.   We needed
the contrasts to see that sooner or later the organisational landscape would have to change.   In this chapter
we shall first explore the reasons for change in
organisations which emerged during the 1960s and 1970s.
Then we shall compare traditional and new organisational
ideas.   An example from the hotel industry will be used
to discuss some main points to bear in mind when a new
organisation is created.   We shall then describe some
basic principles which can be used to move towards new
forms of organisation, the matrix principle, self-
managing work groups, etc.   Finally we shall discuss
the new roles of supervisors, specialists and managers.

1.   <u>Why did basic changes in
     the organisation of work
     emerge during the 1960s
     and 1970s?</u>

<u>First, a basic change in technology</u> started to have
an effect upon the organisation of work.   As long as
mechanisation was a major feature of technological
change in industry the organisational patterns developed
correspondingly.   Increased mechanisation, based on a
high degree of standardisation of products and methods,
led to increased specialisation of work.   This, in turn,
led to reduced needs for the training of workers, since
knowledge, co-ordination and control were moved from the
shop floor to the office, from the worker to the staff
specialist.   The person became an "exchangeable part"
in the organisational machinery.   Planning and the control of quality and cost were centralised.   This made
some sort of sense if one could afford to overlook the
social and psychological disadvantages.   In spite of all
sorts of economic incentives and promotion schemes this
became increasingly difficult.

When <u>automation</u> started to replace mechanisation as
the new form of technology, this led to new demands for
decentralised control systems.   Within these systems
people could not be treated as replaceable parts.   They
had to make decisions that could not be programmed.
Their major functions would be to learn, to judge and to
act responsibly.   Their major functions would not be to

4

feed and handle machinery as they would have been when mechanisation was the major feature of technology.

The fragmentation of jobs, which seemed logical when co-ordination and control had been centralised, made little sense when operator and staff were required to understand and control the whole process of production. Narrow jobs and closed careers prevented the integration of production and maintenance, a crucial requirement of the new technology of the 1960s and 1970s.

Mass production and mass distribution had caused organisations to grow in size. The economy of size - the bigger the better - had been taken for granted as being effective also in service institutions. It became slowly evident that mechanisation and size were accompanied by a third principle, namely bureaucratisation. Job fragmentation and centralised control required complex rules and regulations. Status barriers became stronger and communication problems were a major concern of all large organisations, particularly in a rapidly growing service sector. As the new technology gradually caused new forms of work organisation to develop, different types of service institutions also turned out to have their own specific needs for change. As the computer started to change administrative technology, non-bureaucratic forms of organisation started to appear not only in industry and commerce but also in public administration, welfare and education. But this was the exception and not the rule.

Second, mass education represented a second force helping to increase organisational changes. When large numbers of unskilled workers had moved from agriculture into industrial mass manufacturing it made some sort of sense to create narrow jobs with little need for education and training. When large numbers of young people with higher education moved into industry and the services in the 1960s and 1970s the narrow jobs no longer made sense. In fact it became increasingly difficult to find people willing to do work that was little but routine. Absenteeism and turnover among employees soared in industry and other branches. This then led to increased pressure to develop new forms of work organisation. However, mass education does not automatically lead to new organisations. It may create "organisation men" with traditional ideas and attitudes.

A third reason for the emergence of new forms of organisation in the 1960s and 1970s was a revolt among young people and women of the industrialised world. Behind this revolt was a change in values slowly emerging among people in general. When the Beatniks and the Hippies rose in protest against the Establishment they

had a sense of new values.   They were "symptoms of a
cultural change".   They sensed the environmental threat,
the energy crisis and the enlarging gap between the rich
and the poor world.   Governmental bureaucracies, big
business and big science paid little attention to any of
this until crisis was looming on the horizon.

Growing unemployment as part of an economic crisis
represents a fourth reason for the emergence of new forms
of work organisation during the 1970s.   The oil shock of
1973-74 turned out to be much more than a single incident.
It was part of a structural change in the economics of
both the industrialised and the developing countries.
When women and young people in rapidly increasing numbers
appeared on the labour market they found a decreasing
number of jobs open to them.   The jobs that were open
held little appeal for them.   Often they were jobs that
had been filled by unskilled foreign labour, now forced
back to the poor world by unemployment in the industrialised countries.

Job sharing, shorter working hours and longer holi-
days have been among the means suggested to reduce
unemployment.   So far there is little proof that such
ideas will work as long as the nature of work organisations remains unchanged.   Rigid, hierarchical organisations do not lend themselves, for example, to flexible
working hours, overlapping work roles or alternation
between different jobs and careers.   This is particularly
true where disadvantaged groups are confronted with
highly professionalised groups protected by the bureaucratic systems of private and public enterprises.

During the 1980s and 1990s the impact of the new
electronic revolution will hit the labour market.   The
educational system will be under strong pressure to
adapt itself to the new technology and the new social
demands.   Job and career patterns will have to change.
More and more work will be computer-based information
handling and programming.   In traditional forms of
organisation this type of work is usually split into
simple routine jobs on the one hand and conceptual and
administrative jobs on the other.   This polarisation of
work creates technical, economic and social problems
which we cannot afford to overlook.   Different forms of
organisation that have been emerging during the 1960s and
1970s and also entirely new forms will be in high demand.
What has been viewed as a threat to the established forms
of work and community life may appear as possible solutions.

New trade union policies have also had an impact on
new forms of work organisation emerging during the 1960s
and 1970s.   In some countries, most notably in Scandinavia

and Australia, the central trade union councils have worked out specific policies and programmes to introduce forms of organisation based on participation and increased autonomy and personal development for the employees. In other countries, like the United States, different unions have taken very different stands in these matters. The United Autoworkers Union has been actively involved in job and organisation redesign, while other unions have maintained the traditional point of view that these are questions to be handled by management alone. In some countries, like West Germany, the unions have concentrated on work environment, ergonomics and on the formal representation of employees in the decision-making bodies of the enterprise.

As the impact of new technology on employment conditions increases, and as job security and safety become more critical to peoples' quality of life, the unions are bound to become more involved in developing new forms of work organisation. This may not only affect the organisation of factories, offices, etc., but also the structure of unions as such. The unions face some of the same problems of bureaucratisation as any other large-scale organisation.

The changing market conditions have had different impacts upon work organisation in different industries. In general, the markets have become less stable particularly after the oil crisis in 1973. Many enterprises have gone out of business because they have not been able to adapt to new price and market demands. In most industries product specialisation has increased and caused corresponding specialisation to take place in methods and job structure. This has in most cases made highly specialised work organisation vulnerable. During the last two decades many enterprises have found that they were required to build learning and change capacity into their work organisation rather than to rely on more permanent allocation of tasks to highly specialised jobs. Contrary to traditional organisational thinking this despecialisation of jobs does not prevent enterprises from coping with specialisation of methods and products.

2. Traditional and new
    organisational ideas

During the 1950s, so-called self-managing or autonomous work groups were studied in British coalmining.[1] With the introduction of the new technology, the miners' jobs had been specialised like those in industrial manufacturing. Productivity did not improve as expected, and accidents, absenteeism and labour turnover increased. Traditionally minders had learned to do several jobs and

to work together in groups with very little supervision.
When they were allowed to organise themselves again in
the more traditional way many of the social problems were
solved and productivity also improved. A similar experience with work groups started to be manifest in industry,
and empirical studies were made to compare work groups
with segmented jobs. The basic question was: What are
the nature and consequences of specialised and monotonous
work? Walker and Guest had studied The man on the
assembly line.[2] Davis and his associates in 1955 made a
survey of job design practices in United States industry.[3]
There were three basic principles:

(i)   maximum specialisation, i.e. in every job each
        worker had only a few tasks or a single task;

(ii) maximum simplification of the tasks of workers,
        i.e. complex tasks like co-ordination and
        planning were not to be performed at the
        workers' level but at some "higher level" in
        the organisation;

(iii) minimum time needed for training workers, i.e.
        workers were not supposed to learn on the job
        but, if necessary, somewhere else.

Behind these job design principles there is a basic
view of man as a worker, which makes him very similar to
a machine. The next step is to see him as part of a
machine and finally to develop an organisation design
principle where men and machines are viewed as "exchangeable parts". It was in the light of this perspective
that one could see The myth of the machine[4] as a long
historical tradition in industrial society. It was the
same perspective that led to a search for alternative
design principles.

Jordan has made a very important observation in his
analysis of man-machine systems.[5] He concludes that men
and machines have not similar but complementary characteristics. Therefore, what machines do well men do not,
for example, repeating heavy or rapid tasks over long
periods of time. On the other hand, what men do well
machines do not, for example making independent judgements
to respond to new situations and learning over time.

Jordan's insight makes it easier to develop alternative job and organisation design principles through the
so-called socio-technical approach. Here the following
principles are essential. First, that jobs, work groups
and organisational units need to be designed according to
task requirements. Since tasks as we find them in modern
production are highly related, for technical reasons or
because a certain sequence or quality needs to be

maintained, such tasks cannot be performed well by people in segmented, unrelated work roles. Or alternatively, these work roles require complex systems of specialist and management co-ordination and control. Once this is understood, it is easier to understand why over-specialised work in industry leaves foremen with an almost impossible job, and why endless conflicts occur between staff and line managers.[6] The further away from workers one puts planning and the control of cost, quality, etc., the more likely information and control are to break down. This is particularly true for modern technology.

A second principle of socio-technical design is that jobs need to fulfil certain psychological and social requirements, besides task demands (and beyond safety, security and wage demands as stated by agreement or law). Consequently, making jobs more meaningful was essential and it was also essential to enable workers to learn more and to exercise control over their own work. Planning and decision making and mutual help and social support were put back into jobs and work groups.

When this socio-technical approach was attempted on a broad basis, as in the Norwegian participation projects,[7] a new basic design principle emerged. This was in complete contrast with the machine theory of scientific management. It was based on building additional functions for learning, planning, etc., into people and organisations. In this context the consequences of the previous trend, "to treat people like exchangeable parts", became more evident. Discussions of industrial conflicts, worker motivation and alienation in industry took on a new perspective. Work itself had to be changed, and not only at the workers' level. Naturally, there would be opposition against the new forms of work organisation. What proof was there that productivity would not suffer? Or that workers and staff were actually willing and able to take more responsibility? Relevant as these questions were - and they had to be answered by evidence from actual experience - they were not the main issues. The crux of the matter was that the basic reasons for change had not been realised: the new technology, higher education, the energy and ecology problems and the slowly changing values among people at work and in society in general.

In some countries like Norway and Sweden, the Netherlands and Australia, the interest in new forms of work organisation grew because they were associated with reforms like workers' participation and industrial democracy. In other countries such concepts caused increased scepticism.

When Herbst reviewed the strategies of change used
in work democratisation projects he realised that the
bureaucratic system as such had been threatened.[8] Opposition to these projects was easier to understand when they
were contrasted with the basic assumptions of bureaucratic, hierarchical design. These assumptions are:

First, that tasks can be decomposed into smaller
and smaller independent bits.

Second, that each person or unit is supposed to perform only one task. The consequences are many and in
sharp contrast with those of self-managing groups and
similar arrangements. The bureaucratic consequences
are that only one single structure can exist between
units. Consequently, only a uniform relation between
people will exist, namely a superior-subordinate one.
Every subordinate reports or "belongs" to one superior.
Furthermore, clearly demarked boundaries are drawn
between the functions of each person and each unit.
Task performance is split from decision making. Those
at the top of hierarchies may be left with no task
performance and those at the bottom with no decision
making at all. When bureaucracy had acquired these
characteristics it was in sharp conflict with the social
and technological trends of the 1970s. This was true
even when its advantage in the "equal treatment" of
people was taken into account.

A third principle of socio-technical design, in fact
the most basic one, is that a work organisation is seen
as an open system, not as a closed one. This means that
changes in the environment of the enterprise, particularly
through market mechanisms, have a continuous impact upon
the organisation and lead to internal changes over time.
The other way around, the organisation also has an impact
upon its environment and influences its markets and the
local community, etc. The rather stable growth in the
markets of most companies of the industrialised world
during the 1960s and 1970s caused most organisations to
continue to produce more of the same or similar products
and to remain basically the same in terms of organisational structure. Particularly after the oil crisis of
1973 and when the full impact of new industrial nations
like Japan had been felt on world-wide trade, the market
situation changed drastically. Most companies were
forced to review their product and price policies as well
as their organisation policy. In this situation many
companies just increased their centralised control;
others understood that differentiation of products and
new forms of organisational integration were needed.
These market changes caused pressure for new forms of
organisations to develop at the same time that the anxiety

caused by an emerging economic crisis made people hesitant to try out new ideas.

Against this background it is not surprising that the diffusion of new forms of organisation, tending towards a non-hierarchical system, was difficult. Neither is it surprising that foremen and specialists engulfed in bureaucratic systems often remained apprehensive of the new forms of organisation until they could see what new roles were open for them. It is not surprising that those who were used to running large organisations from the top of a hierarchy were sometimes sceptical. This was true fo a large number of influential leaders of private and public enterprises, of governmental agencies and of many large trade unions.

In retrospect we can see many reasons why very much the same old organisation structure is still to be found everywhere, in spite of strong pressures for change, and in spite of the new alternatives that have been developing during the 1960s and 1970s. Some of the main reasons are:

    (i)   The traditional forms were quite suitable to the main technological trend, mechanisation, and it took time, after 1960, to realise that the shift to process - and electronic - technology required new forms.

    (ii)   The effectiveness of large-scale, hierarchical organisations was measured in simple economic terms that did not reveal their wastage of energy and human resources and their threat to ecologic balance. It is only recently that we have begun to realise that we cannot afford this.

    (iii)   Traditional forms of organisation protected the privileges of people with power and high status. This was true not only of owners, members of management and highly educated specialists but also of groups of privileged workers and staff.

    (iv)   The traditional forms "condition" or teach people to accept what they see all around. With time, people stop looking for alternatives. Those who have privileged positions find good reasons why they need them or deserve them. Those who have not, learn to live with the situation.

    (v)   The traditional forms include payment systems, planning and administrative routines etc., which need to be adjusted to new forms of

organisation. When these adjustments take place
uncertainty may arise about how managerial control is maintained. This may be the case even
when the new forms are designed to reduce the
needs for internal co-ordination and control
and enable management to concentrate on the
more important control of the inter-action between the organisation and the outside world.

(vi) It takes time to develop new forms of organisation. Before the necessary conditions for new
forms are established, people often give up and
return to "the devil they know" rather than
take risks with the unknown.

To develop new forms of organisation is obviously
not a simple matter. To come to grips with concrete
measures we shall take a closer look at a specific
industry, the hotel industry. People working with
organisations generally know something about hotels and
should be able to see that most of the principal points
are relevant also to other branches. But first let us
summarise and be clear about traditional organisations,
we shall call them "uniform" organisations, and differen-
tiate between them and alternative forms of organisations
which we shall call multiform.

3. Creating a new form of organisation
    in a changing environment: An
    example from the hotel industry

If we are introduced to a well established form of
work organisation as strangers it is not so easy to understand what makes it tick. However, a naive outsider who
starts to suggest changes soon finds out that matters are
not as simple as they appear to be. If you want to
change work allocation "it can't be done" because labour
contracts define jobs and tie them to specific training,
pay, promotion, etc. If you want to change technology
you may have to change the recruitment and training of
workers and staff. It becomes clear that each part of
the organisation is tied up with other parts. Equally
important, internal elements are linked to others outside. Organisations exist in an environment, not in a
vacuum. Only naive outsiders treat organisations as
simple machines, where repairs are made by putting in
exchangeable parts.

Many specialists and managers have been allowed to
treat organisations as machines. Some organisations
have in fact become like machines because of the way they
are maintained by managers and specialists who come and

12

Contrasts between main types of organisation

Traditional "uniform" type	Multiform type
1. Tasks broken down into unrelated bits.	Tasks vary in complexity and kept as "complete wholes".
2. Job training and knowledge are minimised.	Training and knowledge are broad and cover future needs.
3. Most workers' jobs repetitive.	Few jobs repetitive.
4. Sharp job demarcations.	Partly overlapping jobs.
5. One person, one job.	Individual or group work.
6. Every person, one boss.	Some report to one, others to more.
7. Groups only "informal".	Groups share responsibility.
8. Task and responsibility relatively permanent.	People may rotate between roles - horizontally and vertically.
9. Information and control mostly vertical, top-down.	Info-control, vertical or horizontal depending on problem situation.
10. Planning and decision making are centralised.	Decentralisation. Planning and decision making part of all jobs.
11. Technology taken as given.	Technology adapted to social and organisational needs.
12. Tall organisation chart.	"Flat" organisation chart.
13. Few links with outside.	Many links with outside.
14. Centralised and little risk taking.	Extensive innovation and risk taking.
15. Design principle: Man as "exchangeable part".	Man and organisation learning to take on new functions.
16. Administrative infrastructure prevents self-regulation.	Infrastructure promotes self-regulation and self-management.

go.   In such cases, we can hardly speak of established work organisations functioning in a changing environment, which is what we shall be concerned with.

If we were to establish a completely new work organisation we should have to consider all the necessary conditions for its functioning - both internal and external conditions.   What are the basic issues we then have to explore?   Let us say that we are members of a project team brought together to establish a new hotel. We obviously have to ask: Who wants it and why?   Soon a number of related questions have to be considered in further detail.

(i) The interest groups involved.   It is important to define the people involved in the initiation of a new project.   Is it a group of owners who have seen a business opportunity or even a single investor?   Is it a group of users, firms, associations or local authorities who have seen the need for the creation of hotel services?   Or is it perhaps some professional people who have wanted to leave their jobs and have seen an opening in the market?

The questions we are raising here concern the institutional and political basis for starting an enterprise and running it successfully.   Without this basis a new project has no protection.   The hotel industry exists within an extended field of tourism, airlines, shipping, national and international firms, holding companies, trade associations, etc.   Who will be the allies and who the competitors of a new enterprise?   There are numerous uncertainties related to the markets, the trade unions and the professions involved.   These uncertainties can be, and need to be, reduced, by establishing some balance of power between the groups involved. Organisations do this through control over investments, through the regulation of purchases and sales, through contracts and through coalitions.

The question raised regarding interest groups cannot be answered fully until we have looked at other aspects of the whole project, including the location and size of the new enterprise.

One may ask what the relative strength of interest groups behind a new hotel has to do with the functioning of work ogranisations in general.   The point is that each group exercises its power according to the type of interest it represents.   Investors are basically concerned with long-term protection and growth of capital. Suppliers are concerned with steady delivery at a good price.   Municipal and governmental authorities are concerned with the integration of firms in public policy.

14

Consumer organisations concentrate on the control of the quality and price of products and services. Trade unions and professional organisations are concerned with job security and conditions of work. Traditionally, it was assumed that the objective of an enterprise could be formulated as the maximisation of profit. This seems to be a basic assumption behind the design of traditional industrial organisations. But this assumption is far too simple to be used for the formulation of organisational goals in the type of societies we are confronted with now. It is more appropriate to define objectives in terms of the relative dependence of an organisation upon the various parts of its environment.

Questions of interdependence cannot be answered only in economic terms, although this is obviously important when one is dealing with different types of markets for raw materials, sales, etc. But questions of trust and social support are equally important. This is true in any branch of economic activity and in any trade or service.

(ii) The location and the size of a work organisation are important for any firm and particularly for a hotel. There is clearly a difference between a tourist hotel in the mountains and a city hotel catering for business people, government officials and similar groups. Location and size are closely inter-related and they are further related to the type and the number of customers aimed at. So the question of location and size has to be left open until other questions have been settled.

It could be asked how important location and size may be in other branches than the hotel industry. Take a paper mill, a transport firm or a dairy. Or take a fertilizer plant, a mechanical repair shop or a post office. In all cases it is fairly obvious that location and size need to be adjusted to specific local conditions. But it is not a matter of a one-way adjustment. Enterprises influence their environment. So what we are concerned with in organisational design is a matter of interdependence between an enterprise and the outside world.

(iii) Distinctive competence. This is largely a question of what one enterprise can do better than others. It is a crucial point in deciding what sort of interdependence is desirable for an enterprise. If it is alone in the market, because of its location, then distinctive competence may not be so important. But not many firms are alone or in full control of their market.

Today, most hotels are specialised, as can be seen
in the way they present themselves to the outside. Their
image is expressed in buildings and furniture and also in
advertising, employment notices, etc. Hotels that try
to be good at everything are usually not really good at
anything.

Is distinctive competence as important in other
branches as it is in the hotel industry? Ask the question in the garment or the furniture industry or in
building and construction. Firms that try to get all
sorts of contracts soon end up by losing them all to
firms that specialise in some area and stay away from
others. The problem is that it is also risky to specialise too much. Firms that expand into new areas with
too broad or too narrow a competence may face failure.
This means more than the loss of investment. It may
mean total ruin.

(iv) <u>The physical facilities and the technology of
the enterprise</u>. A modern city hotel has a highly sophisticated technology. Materials used for building and
maintenance require specialists of all kinds and supply
from a large number of firms, quite often in a foreign
country. The electronic revolution makes a modern
hotel highly dependent on computer booking services,
often within an international network. The heating and
cooling systems require the stable delivery of expensive
energy and maintenance skills equal to those of a modern
ship. All these aspects of technology in a hotel have
an influence upon organisational design.

If choice of technology is important in a hotel, it
is even more so in other branches such as those mentioned.
Take a steel plant or a paper plant, a newspaper or a
shipyard, a machine factory or a computer firm. What is
particularly important for organisational design is that
the possibility of <u>choice</u> between types and levels of
technology has greatly increased over the last few years.
Simultaneously the cost of energy and labour required by
different technologies has changed drastically.

(v) <u>Organisational structure, the climate and the
people</u>. Having moved from one issue to the other, from
the institutional or political support to financing,
from distinctive competence to technology, we are back
to the human and organisational side of the enterprise.
What sort of people in what kind of work roles are needed?
What is needed may not be easily available. What is
available may not be suitable any more for present and
future needs.

Traditionally a hotel manager would be able to recruit and train the people he needs for the main roles of cook, waiter, chamber maid, receptionist, etc. Quite often the family owning a hotel would cover most of the main work roles. Local people might be hired when needed and not working on their farms, in private households or elsewhere. Perhaps this tradition will be revived in the hotel industry and other branches when the labour market changes and when the value of local communities are better understood.

In a modern hotel, most of the traditional roles still exist but recruitment has changed completely. It takes place in a partly national, partly international labour market. Some employees are highly professional and conscious of status and role. Others are young people or housewives taking a job to make some extra money or for finding out what kinds of work they like. Many are unskilled and come from poor countries; they may have a few rights and little protection at home and abroad. In such a situation having a personnel policy is essential if one is going to develop an organisation systematically.

In most countries new personnel policies will have to be considered in the context of new labour law and the system of labour-management bargaining. This is the case in hotels as well as in other industries. The trade unions play an essential role in the institutional, political network any new enterprise must take into account when it wants to establish itself as a part of modern society.

Different organisations need different types of leadership. If a hotel is highly specialised, this tends to create a corresponding type of leadership and social atmosphere. Some hotels, depending on size, tradition, etc., operate very much like a unit of the army or a ship. These are typical "uniform" types of organisation. Other hotels operate more like families. Which of the two types has the better work organisation and atmosphere depends on the sort of hotel we are referring to. We have to turn back to the basic questions we raised initially: What groups and institutions have a stake in the enterprise? In what markets and local environment does it operate? Does it offer the services needed and preferred by the public it caters for? We have now come to a series of issues that we refer to as policy questions.

The main point we have been trying to make so far is that the design of a new hotel and its work organisation are matters of choice. And this is true of any work organisation.

Policy is sometimes determined as though it were a matter of gathering facts and drawing the conclusion. This is only part of it. Policy making is much more complex. For people to accept policy as valid guidelines for critical decisions, which is what it is supposed to be, takes time. Policy making requires a knowledge of culture and a sense of values if it is to form a common basis for judging what is right or wrong in organisational life.

If policy is determined by one or a few people at the top of the organisation and enforced down the line, this may be an effective way of creating one type of structure, a traditional hierarchical one. If policy is determined by a passive acceptance of minimal rules and regulatinns from outside, this leads to a different structure - probably one where most things are left to chance. If policy making takes the form of a step-by-step learning process where those affected by the policy and expected to live by it are involved, this creates a different structure again. This type of structure has a built-in capacity to adapt the organisation continuously to changing demands. Selznick has described how different types of leadership and organisational climate depend on the policy-making process.[9] We shall return to this matter as a critical issue when we discuss different ways of changing organisations.

We may sum up at this point by putting together the main factors we have discussed in relation to the starting of an organisation from scratch. The same factors have to be considered if we want to make a conscious change in any existing work organisation. We do not pretend to have dealt with all the relevant factors. We have been trying to make the point that we are dealing with an organisational system where the parts are intimately related to each other. The parts exist both inside and outside the boundaries of the organisation. On the basis of this overview we shall go back to the basic problem of how to develop alternatives to uniform organisation.

4. Changing from uniform to multiform type of organisation

If we consider the experience of the last 20 years we will find that there are at least two ways of moving away from the traditional hierarchical, uniform type of organisation.[8] One is to design overlapping jobs in what is called a matrix organisation. The other is to create self-managing work groups.

18

Figure 1 Showing the interrelations between internal and external parts of an organisation

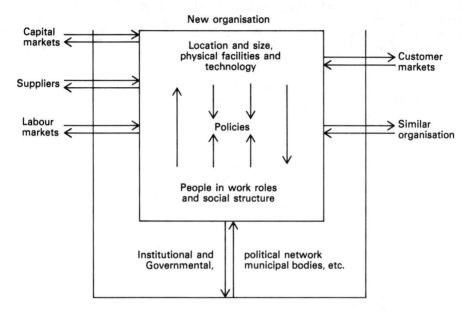

The matrix principle

Matrix organisation is based on two principles opposed to that of uniform, hierarchical organisation. Each person is assumed to cover more than one work role. And each person is assumed to alternate between different roles and status levels. The overlapping between roles is limited because some degree of specialisation is required. In the following structure, each of the persons can perform two to four different jobs apart from his own.

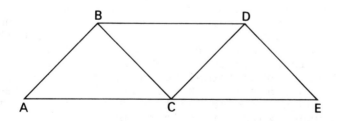

Person A can alternate with B and C because of overlapping competence, but not with D and E.   C can alternate with A, B, D and E.   This means that in the matrix, <u>one basic structure exists when all the people are performing their main roles</u>.   When they are not, a number of alternative work relations can be established.

In a uniform, hierarchical organisation the five jobs might be related as follows:

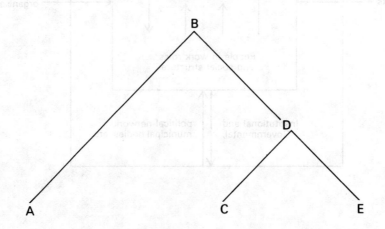

Since persons in this type of structure are usually not supposed to alternate between status levels, we can immediately see that the latter structure is quite dependent on "spare parts".   If one person is absent, replacement from outside is necessary.

The informal use of matrix principles takes place in most organisations in a very simple way.   People who work close to each other know enough about each other's work to be able to stand in for each other.   Informal training for this usually occurs when people help each other.   Or one job is the stepping-stone to another. In a bureaucratic system the matrix principle usually does not work because roles are strictly defined, and people at one status level cannot, or will not, work at another.   Even if roles are at the same level difficulties occur, since alternation depends on co-ordination from above or on some formal decision or agreement. Matrix alternation will work well only if it is pre-arranged through training and through agreement on the conditions under which it is to be used.

In the process industry matrix alternation is often used during repair or maintenance.   A process worker may be trained and have a secondary role to play when certain repairs take place.   He may then work under a skilled maintenance specialist.   When repairs are done he moves back to his process work and the maintenance man moves on to different maintenance jobs and occasionally to some sort of process control.

In banks the matrix system is often used to cope with variations in workload in different parts of the bank - during rush hours, on paydays, etc.   Again, this is dependent on systematic training and agreement on conditions.   An important point is also the definition of responsibility.   An important distinction sometimes has to be made between accountability and responsibility. A number of cashiers and clerks may take joint responsibility for attending to certain services for certain customers in a branch office.   They will be accountable on an individual basis according to procedures of signature.   In other types of work accountability may be defined in relation to budget, expenditure or similar variables.

In professional groups the matrix system is particularly relevant.   In some cases this may involve more than one organisation, for example, a technical specialist may have a staff role or a consultant role to play in an organisation when certain tasks have to be performed.   When the tasks can be handled without the external specialist he moves back to a semi-permanent role in his own organisation.   Training, payment and other conditions for this arrangement need to be agreed upon by the two organisations.

In recent field experiments in the Norwegian merchant navy an efficient and safe type of matrix organisation was developed by the people on board a project ship.[10]   This was based on the multipurpose training of deck and engine personnel.   Some of the crew acquired certificates for more than one deparment.   This arrangement has since formed the basis for significant changes in the training of seafarers, in new manning regulations and in the career system.   A matrix system will broaden the career and make it easier to change from one career to another at sea and also from sea to shore. This may be of increasing importance in a period of rapid technological and social change (see figure 2).

We can easily see that in the uniform type of organisation variation in tasks is more limited than in the matrix form.   Learning on the job is likely to be less demanding and consequently the future of persons in uniform jobs is less open.

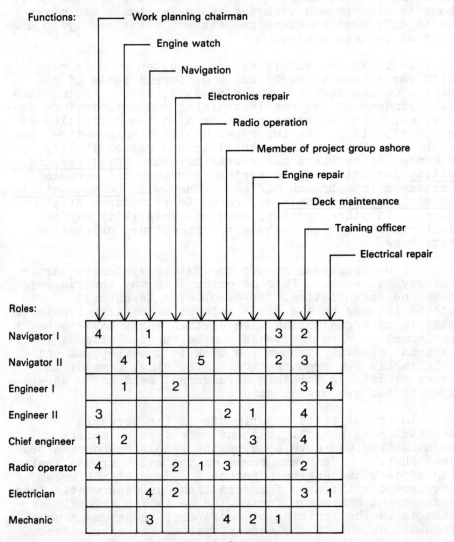

Figure 2   Example of matrix organisation for a ship

Functions:
- Work planning chairman
- Engine watch
- Navigation
- Electronics repair
- Radio operation
- Member of project group ashore
- Engine repair
- Deck maintenance
- Training officer
- Electrical repair

Roles:

	Work planning chairman	Engine watch	Navigation	Electronics repair	Radio operation	Member of project group ashore	Engine repair	Deck maintenance	Training officer	Electrical repair
Navigator I	4		1					3	2	
Navigator II		4	1		5			2	3	
Engineer I		1		2					3	4
Engineer II	3					2	1		4	
Chief engineer	1	2					3		4	
Radio operator	4			2	1	3			2	
Electrician			4	2					3	1
Mechanic			3				4	2	1	

1 means primary role, 2 secondary, etc.

In this ship several members of the crew hold certificates outside their own department (dual junior officer training).

In the matrix type of structure several people can share the responsibility for a complex set of tasks. In the hierarchical, uniform type, one and only one person is assumed to be responsible and accountable for all tasks within a certain area. For example, a maintenance foreman may be formally responsible for a group of skilled mechanics and a plumber and an electrician who carry out day-to-day repairs and maintenance on a production line. If the foreman has a vocational background as a mechanic he can to some extent take the responsibility for mechanical repairs, but he has to spend a lot of time on control of his subordinates; however, when plumbing and electrical jobs are done he has to rely on the responsibility of those skilled in such work. In a matrix system the maintenance team may reorganise itself according to the nature of each major job to be done. If a repair job primarily requires the knowledge of an electrician he will take the responsibility for that job, while a mechanic and a plumber may assist him. If the job is basically of a mechanical nature, the mechanic will take the responsibility while the electrician and the plumber act as his helpers to dismantle the machinery, etc. This does not prevent a foreman from being accountable for the budgeting and the cost control of the maintenance. In the matrix system the foreman may also join a group under the responsibility of one of the specialist workers and act as one of his "assistants".

This example raises two important questions. One is that the matrix system should not be used in such a way that a skilled worker or a specialist loses his professional identity. He must not be considered as a "jack of all trades" because he works together with other professions. This can be avoided through the type of contract given to members of a matrix organisation, not only regarding pay but also responsibilities, job security, time for further training, lines of promotion, etc. A second question, closely related to the first one, is how trade union contracts can cover matrix forms of work organisation on the central (national) as well as the enterprise levels. Traditionally labour contracts would be based on very precise definitions of tasks and jobs and related pay and working conditions. This is no longer possible when enterprises have to change very frequently their methods, technology, etc. In this situation the contracts need to cover general job competence and responsibilities and minimum pay for different broad categories. This is usually achieved through basic contracts covering a national union and local modifications settled through decentralised bargaining at the company level. In practice it turns out to be easier for specialists at all levels to maintain their competence when they work in matrix organisations. The

more people have an opportunity to renew their skills and
knowledge the more willing and able they are to use the
matrix system.

The concept of the organisational matrix carries
another meaning than the one we have discussed here.
Emery refers to it as a system in which one organisation
can fill the role of another.[11]   This matrix principle
is of great importance, particularly in an unpredictable
environment.   One example is that of the international
communications system.

Self-managing work groups

The systematic study of autonomous work groups took
a major step forward in the 1950s when the Tavistock
Institute became involved in the British mining industry.
Trist and his associates[1] and Herbst[12] outlined the basic
principles of group functioning.   Emery had already
analysed the socio-technical systems background.[13]   But
it should be borne in mind that it was the miners themselves who started to work in what were called composite
or autonomous work groups.   The concept "self-managing
groups" has been found to be a better name, since it is
the group's ability to manage its own affairs and its
relations with the outside that are the most important.

The coalminers "re-invented" a system similar to
that of traditional mining as they knew it.   Rice had
tested out some of the same group principles in the
Indian textile industry.   His experiment did not go much
beyond the matrix principle.   There was some rotation but
little sharing of responsibility.   This was the main reason why development did not continue on the basis of
experience gained over time.   One old system had been
replaced by one new system.   Change capacity had not been
built into the work organisation.   The "experimental
shed" was run very much the same way in 1978 as in 1958.

When group experiments were started in Norwegian
industry in 1964 there were good reasons to believe that
group systems could be an effective way for workers to
participate actively in the control of their own work
situations.[15]   This objective was considered by many to
be ideological or political and to have no place in
industry, quite apart from the fact that there was considerable doubt about how far most workers would be
interested in participation.   When this myth had been
destroyed and the first experiments were over, there were
still major problems of diffusion.   An important reason
for this was the way in which the field experiments were
initiated and organised, particularly the way evaluation
took place.   It was perhaps necessary to use the concept

of an experiment in 1964, since there was a need for
demonstration projects.   Later this became a problem,
because many workers and others had difficulty in taking
over the "ownership" of the project.   Yet this is necessary if matrix groups or self-managing work groups are
to continue their own development.

The task structure of self-managing groups will, in
the extreme case, be as follows:

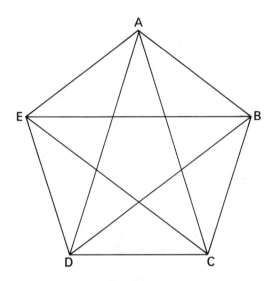

All the five members A, B, C, D and E can take on all
the five major tasks (or work roles).   One of them will,
on a rotation basis, act as a contact person with the
outside, as one part of his or her role.   A total rotation and changeability of people and tasks is in most
cases not technologically or socially feasible.   On the
other hand, too little rotation will soon reduce the
learning and communication below the level necessary for
the group to keep up its own autonomous functioning and
its further development.

A standard objection to the use of the group principle is that a group cannot take responsibility, which
can be taken only by one person in a particular type of
role.   This is logical if one assumes that most tasks
and jobs are narrow, that they are not related to each
other, and that performance needs to be split from co-
ordination and control.   This is not true of self-
managing groups.   The basis is that a group task exists,
since the tasks are inter-related and form a whole that
the members of the group can identify as their joint
responsibility, which they are able and willing to take

25

on together.   This works only if the necessary training
takes place, if information, equipment, etc., are available to the group and an agreement is set up between the
group and the rest of the organisation.

The confusion about responsibility and accountability is one reason for rejecting group work.   However,
quite often there is a much deeper reason.   People who
are attuned to uniform organisations find it almost
irresponsible to talk about sharing responsibility. Yet
they know that they cannot control all the activities in
a modern work organisation.   According to their own
principles they cannot take responsibility for what they
cannot control.   However, most people in uniform
organisations have learned how to live with this sort of
contradiction.   Foremen and supervisors have the biggest
trouble, since they face the contradiction daily.   No
wonder their role has been so well described under the
title "Master and victim of double talk".   Those who
have moved from a uniform to an alternative type of
organisation see matters quite differently.   A sea
captain who had been master of a ship changing its work
organisation to include matrix groups and self-managing
groups was asked: "Who is responsible for safety in
your ship?   Who goes to court if you have a serious
accident?"   He answered: "Everybody is responsible for
safety.   That is why we have fewer accidents than before.
In the case of a serious accident, of course I will go to
court because I am accountable for the ship's operations.
But I should be crazy if I tried to run a modern ship as
if we were in court all the time."

We shall not try to report the results of projects
with self-managing groups.   The literature on this
topic is now abundant.[17]   It may be more relevant to sum
up what turned out to be the main steps in practice, when
group systems were established in manufacturing industry.[18]

(a)   Multi-skilling of operators so that they can change
       between different work roles inside work groups.
       (This is usually needed because of the prevalent
       philosophy of "one man, one skill".)

(b)   Development of an information system including
       measuring of variations needed for control by
       operators.   This is often necessary because con-
       trol has been traditionally held at a level far
       removed from action.   In one case the establish-
       ment of a new information room was a major element
       in one phase of an experiment.   Involvement in
       data analysis is a good way of training the groups.

26

(c) Attachment of a local repair man to back up the quick and detailed control actions for which the operators are expected to assume responsibility. The integration of maintenance and daily operations can be organised in many ways.

(d) Institutionalising the meetings, contacts, etc., that enable the operators, as a group, to plan and co-ordinate their activities. Orderly contact between groups and the rest of the organisation must develop over time.

(e) Training the foremen to supervise, co-ordinate and plan for the activities of groups rather than individuals. This usually means an extension of their time span of responsibility and some skilling in tasks of appraisal, diagnosis and production planning that are traditionally located at the middle-management level.

(f) Design and introduction of new bonus arrangements, if the department has or needs some special kind of incentive schemes.

(g) Periodic review and evaluation of group performance is necessary both for adjustments to be made in the groups and for new contracts to be set up between the groups and the organisation.

This list is not complete and it will vary according to the tasks involved and the rest of the organisation structure. One way of getting insight into the structure and functioning of groups is to look at the basic conditions enabling groups to maintain their self-management capacity. The following conditions are usually necessary but may not be sufficient in all cases.[19]

(1) Are the boundary conditions, inputs and outputs, of the group relatively stable so that some sort of group contract can be established? (Rather than very unstable.)

(2) Will the primary task of the group consist of a set of interdependent subtasks which make up a meaningful whole task? (Rather than independent subtasks.)

(3) Will the control over secondary tasks (like maintenance, planning, etc.) be partly up to the groups?

(4) Does the group decide who does what? (Rather than being told by the supervisor.)

(5) Do group members have sufficient knowledge to handle the group task? (Rather than depending on outsiders.)

(6) Has the group its own tools and equipment?

(7) Is external leadership based on group sanctioning? (Rather than being imposed upon the group.)

(8) Is some degree of self-recruitment left to the group?

(9) Has the group a territory of its own?

(10) Are the incentives on group level? (Rather than on individual level.)

None of these conditions can be fulfilled 100 per cent. If several of them are not or are hardly fulfilled the chances of maintaining the self-management capacity are low. Gulowsen has used some of these conditions as a measure of group autonomy.[20]

5. The supervisory level
under restructuring

Groups of workers cannot manage themselves if the traditional roles of supervisors remain unchanged. When some basic conditions for self-management in groups are fulfilled inside the groups, the necessary conditions outside, on their boundaries, clearly come to the surface. For example, when sufficient training has been given to operators and when they have the necessary information, tools and other resources, they are usually both willing and able to accept responsibility for the group task. This task will have to be challenging enough for the group to take pride in it and for members to grow with it. Consequently, a fair amount of planning, and perhaps quality control and some maintenance and other auxiliary tasks, will be delegated to the group. Then, and only then, will the group be willing to take over internal co-ordination - to decide who does what, how to help each other and how to discipline each other if necessary. When this has taken place, the group has already become involved in supervisory and managerial functions and starts raising its sights, asking, for instance:

- Why are materials not available as prescribed? We gave notice that we should soon run out of parts; why is the delivery system not working? (To involve group members in project groups to help to improve the supply system is often very effective.)

28

- Why is the maintenance service not working as it
  should? We said that we should soon have a break-
  down if the repair man did not come. Why can't
  we call him and get him here quickly? He knows
  what to do. (Again, to involve group members
  together with supervisors in the improvement of
  maintenance is useful, but obviously the outside
  specialists need to take a leading role here.)

- Why is the quality of deliveries below standard?
  We have complained several times that the parts vary
  too much, exceeding the tolerances agreed upon.
  (When groups get involved in these questions it
  simply means that quality is under better control
  and the control system can be developed continuously.)

These and similar questions point to the kind of
change the groups expect in supervisory, specialist and
managerial functions. They expect management to concentrate on co-ordination between departments and leave
internal co-ordination and control to the groups - under
normal conditions. They are in fact helping supervisors
and managers to carry out their primary tasks.

The types of change necessary to make group systems
function are also necessary when a matrix system of work
roles is introduced.

6.   Changes in the role of foremen

In the earlier field experiments where self-managing
groups were introduced, many foremen felt threatened.
They feared that there would be no place for them in the
new forms of work organisation. If they had in mind to
maintain the traditional role of the foreman, the over-
seer, the man who knew everything and decided everything
in his unit, their fear was well-grounded. In fact,
that role was already disappearing with the introduction
of more sophisticated technology monitored by workers
who knew more about it and who were often better
educated than their foremen. The old role had dis-
appeared also because specialists had taken over many of
the functions previously covered by the foreman. If
workers did not know how to solve technical problems the
foreman would not know either and he often knew less than
the worker how to present the problems to specialists.

Finally, the old role of the foreman no longer
existed because many of the personnel problems he used to
decide, basing himself on personal judgement, were now
covered by union-management contracts or by policy
guidelines.

But there would still be a number of tasks that self-managing groups and more independent workers could not solve alone. If the foreman and supervisors took over these tasks they would actually work themselves into middle management.

What would this require?

- The primary task of foremen would change from internal co-ordination and control within departments to team work at the horizontal level between departments. This would usually provide more challenging and rewarding jobs. Since the foremen were no longer tied to their own production unit, they would often benefit from moving into a common office area where communication between departments would flow naturally and where team work could develop. Foremen and supervisors could more easily replace each other and therefore be more free to join "task forces" or project groups set up with members from several departments and different levels of the organisation.

- Under the new conditions foremen and supervisors would have to spend much more time on planning and need to know more about it. They would also become more involved in improving the system of maintenance, quality control, transport, storing and other service activities.

- Foremen and supervisors would have to extend their time perspective from perhaps a couple of days to several weeks or even months. Seasonal variations and transfers from one type of product to another would be their primary concern, whereas daily or perhaps weekly variations would be handled by the workers.

- The team work nature of supervision would mean that the vertical form of information and control, characteristic of uniform organisations, would shift to horizontal and functional control.

- This would bring foremen and supervisors into middle management. The so-called foreman problem would disappear. There would no longer be a foreman squeezed between management and the workers. There would be no "master and victim of double talk". This shift would be of such fundamental nature that new concepts would develop to give names to the new type of work relations.

In the process industry, "shift centres" might be established to furnish the shift groups of workers and specialist workers (often working in matrix) with nearly complete management and specialist back-up. In such a centre, covering all shifts and several departments, one might find one or two previous supervisors, mainly concerned with planning, maybe a laboratory worker, a process technician and perhaps a multi-skilled operator who might help out all over the shop floor and perhaps also do simple repairs. This process worker might be a member only for a limited period and then be replaced by another. The technician and the planners might easily leave the centre for a while and work in outside project groups or "task force groups".

In line and batch production, one may find so-called "link groups". These may consist of one or two previous foremen and a multi-skilled operator able to stand in anywhere in the department and perhaps be mainly concerned with training. Finally, there may be a production technician and perhaps a quality specialist. The multi-skilled worker may serve in the link group only for a period and then move back to the shop floor, while a new worker joins the group. Other members of the link group may easily join a project group or a task force to do development work of a varied nature.

Having stated what may happen to supervision when self-managing groups or similar arrangements are introduced at the workers' level, one might well ask: "Should these changes in supervision not be made first, to create conditions for effective self-management at the workers' level?" Logically, the answer is yes, but in practice supervisors and managers are often so heavily burdened with details that they are not able to change their roles before workers relieve them of part of their jobs. Then, and perhaps only then, do they get time and elbow-room to start reorganising their work.

There is a reason, in addition to lack of time, for introducing changes at the workers' level. First, it is difficult to say for sure and in advance what changes at the managerial level will be needed to support changes at the workers' level. This may vary considerably from one situation to the next. It should be understood however that basic change away from the uniform organisation will have to be rooted in the task requirements and not in some abstract theory of management.

In so-called participant redesign workshops (to be discussed elsewhere) the changes in worker-supervisory-managerial levels are planned and carried out simultaneously. A group of people usually from three levels of

the same unit within the organisation, work together on
joint problems, including basic organisational change.
(This type of group is called "vertical slice group"
since it cuts through several levels.)

7.   The role of the specialist
      in alternative structures

      The specialists as well will have to change their
roles if self-managing work groups are to function, or
similar forms of decentralisation to take place in an
effective way.   When supervision changes in the direction
indicated, the watertight partitions between production
departments tend to disappear.   But this is not enough.
Groups of workers and the supervisors will soon face
problems if the specialist departments do not co-operate.
Problems like these come up:

  - Why cannot the planning and the purchasing depart-
    ments co-ordinate their duties in time, so that
    production can flow normally without a last-minute
    rush?   The planning of work is perhaps the most
    important element in this context.   Most of the
    successful cases of reorganisation of work start
    with building planning capacity into workers' roles
    and into the group task of workers and supervisors.

  - Another question that is often raised by self-
    managing production groups is the following: Why
    cannot product designers, purchasing and quality
    control specialists consult production units in
    time?   If production departments are to have a
    chance to voice their opinions and to consider new
    production methods, re-tooling and the training and
    transfer of people, they need time and information.
    This information must flow horizontally as well as
    vertically and must not be used as part of the power
    game between specialists, service departments and
    ambitious individuals.

  - Why cannot maintenance, transport and the laboratory
    departments be attuned more adequately to production
    needs?   ("Do they live a life of their own?")
    The reason why this question often remains unanswered
    is that service departments grow too rapidly when
    responsibility is taken out of workers' jobs.   When
    it is given back to the workers the service depart-
    ments have to change accordingly.

  - Why cannot sales and planning bring their rush
    orders earlier and consult more before regular and
    long-term planning takes place?   This problem can

often be solved when supervisors leave their main
roles and move into task forces and ad hoc groups
to solve special problems in sales and product
development.

-   Why do specialist departments "sit" on their
    information when production departments need to
    share it? This problem can usually be solved when
    workers take over part of what used to be the
    specialists' responsibility and the specialists
    learn that their jobs are moving in the direction
    of a more demanding content. In the transition
    from segmented, hierarchical forms of organisation
    to new forms, specialist departments often tend to
    reject most of these ideas.

In this process, resistance by highly educated
specialists may suggest the need to take a new look at
the education of specialists. There are many ways in
which specialists can work themselves out of the uniform
type of organisation. When there are enough examples
of this, it becomes easier for the educational institutions to change from their uniform type of programmes.

-   Specialists can spend more time on training and
    development work together with other groups (also
    on the shop floor). They can thus leave some of
    their less sophisticated work to non-specialists
    and improve group self-reliance.

-   They can get more time and more opportunities to
    contact outside specialists and keep up their know-
    how and professional network. In some cases they
    may be allowed to take part-time "adjunct" jobs
    outside their own organisation to the benefit of
    more than one organisation.

-   They can have a better opportunity to enter internal
    project groups and get their points of view across
    before other specialists or top management take too
    many decisions.

Several concepts are useful in clarifying the new
roles of specialists. Project groups have already been
mentioned. These should not be confused with committees.
The latter have members who usually maintain their jobs
in permanent positions. Project group members leave
their main job for some time to serve in project groups.
"Task forces" are sometimes used as a name for a similar
arrangement.

A matrix organisation can also be a way for specialists to move into non-hierarchical form of organisation.
In this each specialist has a second or perhaps a third

role to fill besides his main role. The matrix system makes it possible for specialists to have "multiple membership" of different organisations ("selective inter- dependence"). Under this a company specialist can have an adjunct position as a consultant, a research worker or a teacher in an outside organisation. These outside engagements will always be selective, in the sense that some organisations are acceptable as collaborating partners and some are not. The selection of such rela- tions is often based on market considerations and on the needs for complementary knowledge, skill, information, etc. Sometimes personal considerations are important, sometimes cultural criteria are the basis for choice. Long-term relations are always based on trust, which means that there must be a great deal of overlapping in values, and at the same time enough difference to bring a certain amount of challenge into relations.

The different forms of non-hierarchical arrangements we have mentioned at the supervisory and specialist levels open up a new perspective. They make it possible and even necessary for everybody "above" the operator's level to come down to the shop floor for periods and really understand what problems look like in everyday practice. This is a perspective going beyond efficiency. It concerns the development of human respect, through personal contact, in a way which is different from that usually found in hierarchical organisations.

We have stated some conditions to be met by special- ists and their departments when alternatives to hier- archical organisation are developed at the workers' level. One might well ask if specialists should not make the first move and create some of the necessary conditions for change. Theoretically the answer is yes, but in practice this is usually not possible or necessary. What we said earlier in respect of supervisors and middle management applies to specialists as well, for they often have difficulty in finding time to make changes in their own roles before they have been relieved of some of their responsibilities. It is also difficult to say before- hand what specific changes are needed at the specialist's level before restructuring has taken place at the worker's level on the basis of task requirements. Perhaps it is also reasonable to assume that managers, supervisors and workers are more used to making the first step towards getting things moving than specialists are. The latter are more concerned with ideal solutions than with compromises. This follows from their primary role, which is to improve methods and techniques within a theoretical context. It does not mean that special- ists are not, or should not be, concerned with practice.

Non-hierarchical forms of organisation will give them a more direct understanding of practice, which in turn will tend to improve their specialist and professional skills.

8. Management under alternative structures

When operators, supervisors and specialists start to work in the ways described above, top management usually has to answer some important questions, for instance:

- Why is it so difficult to get the necessary decisions to enable middle management to optimise the resources available (people, materials, equipment)?

- Why does not top management clarify the direction in which the organisation is moving to meet the requirements of a changing environment (markets, technology, new social values, etc.)? Without a sense of direction people in the organisation cannot take responsibility for their own work in a way that serves the organisation in the long run.

- Why does top management interfere so frequently with internal co-ordination and the control of matters that it can know only superficially, while more important matters are not attended to?

In the transition from hierarchical forms of organisation to more flexible forms, top management has to make the first move. It must make it clear that the old system will come to an end - and explain why. It must at least create enough free space for members of the organisation to work constructively on proposals that may point out the direction in which the organisation needs to move to cope with external and internal requirements.

To set objectives for their organisation is supposed to be a primary task of management. However, target setting in hierarchical organisations easily deteriorates into mechanical exercises. This becomes part of an internal power game to acquire resources and to avoid the risk of not meeting the expectations of superiors.

What is the alternative to this departmental and individual competition in target setting and the allocation of resources? It follows from the principles of hierarchical organisation that managers at the intermediate level are oriented upwards for power and resources and downwards for control. If one moves towards non-hierarchical organisation, middle management tends to concentrate on <u>horizontal co-ordination</u> or <u>boundary control</u> between departments. (Just like supervisors as indicated above.) This means that middle management works out common targets and budgets and makes readjustments on a collaborative basis when situations change. Obviously top management also has a major role to play in this process. It will have to insist on dealing with co-ordinated and not competitive proposals. This means that middle management will have a team task and not primarily an individual job or position to fill. This can take place only if top management discourage any attempt by individuals to get privileges for their own departments or for themselves.

Is group management viable? Does it not reduce initiative and sense of responsibility? It obviously is viable in many organisations that have changed their management and organisational philosophy. In these organisations, top management also operates as a team. This does not mean that decisions are taken by majority vote. However, if top management continuously suspects that group loyalty will not function in the best interests of the organisation, this becomes a self-fulfilling hypothesis. Middle management learns to concentrate on individual or departmental interests and this has its effect right down to the shop floor. Management itself tends to break into fractions, and cliques are formed.

What practical means do leaders apply when they want to promote organisational growth and adaptation to change? First, they realise that rigid goals in a changing environment are dysfunctional. Just as they know clear goals are relevant in a stable environment. This means that they no longer concentrate on specific objectives to be passed on down the line. Second, they see their primary task as judging constantly the vital <u>interdependencies with the outside environment</u>. They look at the inputs of capital, raw materials, technology, know-how, etc. and their output of products or services. They judge their community relations and make long-term contracts or agreements with major actors in the field their organisation lives in. On this basis they achieve organisational and <u>institutional support</u> from outside on which all members of the organisation can rely ("selective interdependence"); and are able to define a broader <u>mission</u> for the organisation, which members can identify with and which outsiders respect. The mission defines the purpose and the usefulness of the organisation in relation to its environment. In traditional organisations, the specific targets become more important than the mission. Means become ends. This is what institutional leadership must avoid, both in handling outside relations and in cultivating the internal organisational climate.

When an organisation works out its basic inter-relations it is also better able to define its "distinctive competence". This means that both members and outsiders know what the particular organisation is competent and organised to do - and what it is not fit to do. The distinctive competence will be expressed in product ("image") and in the norms for dealing with customers and clients. It defines what "territory" the organisation will serve and protect. Others will have to respect this or enter into conflicts. Organisations with a distinctive competence are not afraid to co-operate with other organisations and leave to them what they are more competent to do. A lack of distinctive competence usually leads to a waste of time and energy in unsuccessful competition in the environment and internal competition for resources for conflicting purposes.

From what has been said about a mission and distinctive competence it follows that non-hierarchical organisations need shared values and agreed norms among their members. To cultivate and protect organisational values and norms and thereby achieve a sense of direction and goal orientation among the members is a major task of top management. It is fully compatible with the other major task, namely to handle the boundary control of the organisation.

Non-hierarchical organisations lose most of the instrumental characteristics of a bureaucracy. The organisation takes on the character of an institution that has values and a mission in itself. It is something more than an instrument to serve the purpose of some higher authority, or having a short-term function in a given market. Leadership in non-hierarchical forms of organisation consequently becomes highly dependent on institutional policy making.

Institutionalisation, however, can create serious inertia in organisations, and it is a major responsibility of members to avoid this. Boundary control means the constant matching of the actual and potential capacities of the organisations to the actual and potential requirements of the environment. If this control is active, then the institutional inertia can be reduced to a tolerable level.

Who will now direct and control the growth of organisations? First of all organisations with distinctive competence tend to redefine growth in many different ways. They do not generally accept expansion as the only, or even the major, form of growth - a rather well-known tendency both for public bureaucracies and private enterprises. Growth may mean the same outputs with lower inputs and less waste, because of higher efficiency in the utilisation of resources. It may mean slightly different types of inputs and outputs through specialisation or differentiation. Institutional leadership in non-hierarchical organisations needs to promote a high degree of self-regulation in the units that make up the whole organisation. It needs to keep up a constant watch and a stepwise valuation and re-distribution of resources to meet changes in its environ-ment.

What we have not discussed in this chapter is the proper use of bureaucratic control to serve other values than organisational growth and adaptation to a changing environment. We should not forget that bureaucracy was introduced to establish reason and fairness where personal power might have been misused. Bureaucracy was meant to protect the individual against the personal whims of an autocratic leader. And it was meant to furnish the rules for the rational handling of matters on the basis of professional knowledge. There are still areas of organisational life where such rules are relevant and useful. But in a rapidly changing society it can hardly be expected to master all the active adaptation needed in organisations to meet the require-ments of the contemporary world of work.

9. References

[1] Trist, E.L., et al.: Organizational Choice (London, Tavistock Publications Ltd., 1963).

[2] Walker, C.R. and Guest, R.H.: The man on the assembly line (Boston, Harvard University Press, 1952).

[3] Davis, L.E., Canter, R.R. and Hoffman, J.: "Current job design criteria", in Journal of Industrial Engineering, Vol. 6, 1955, No. 2.

[4] Mumford, L.: The myth of the machine (London, Secker and Warburg, 1967).

[5] Jordan, J.: "Characteristics of men and machines", in Journal of Applied Psychology, 1963, No. 47.

[6] Dalton, M.: "Conflicts between staff and line managerial officers", in American Sociological Review, 1950, Vol. 15.

[7] Emery, F.E. and Thursrud, E.: Form and content of industrial democracy (London, Tavistock Publications Ltd., 1969).

[8] Herbst, P.G.: Alternatives to hierarchies (Boston, Nijhof, 1976).

[9] Selznic, P.: Leadership in administration (New York, Harper and Row, 1957).

[10] Herbst, P.G.: Socio-technical design (London, Tavistock Publications Ltd., 1974).

[11] Emery, F.E.: Futures we are in (Boston, Nijhof, 1977).

[12] Herbst, P.G.: Autonomous group functioning (London, Tavistock Publications Ltd., 1962).

[13] Emery, F.E.: "Characteristics of socio-technical systems", in The emergence of a new paradigm of work (Canberra, Centre for Continuing Education, Australian National University, 1959).

[14] Rice, A.K.: Productivity and social organization: The Ahmedabad experiment (London, Tavistock Publications Ltd., 1958).

[15] Emery, F.E. and Thorsrud, E.: Democracy at work (Boston, Nijhof, 1976).

[16] McGregor, D.: The human side of the enterprise (New York, McGraw Hill, 1960).

[17] ILO: Bibliography on major aspects of the humanisation of work and the quality of working life (Geneva, ILO, 1978).

[18] Emery, F.E. and Thorsrud, E.: Democracy at work, op. cit.

[19] Thorsrud, E.: "Norwegian experiences with non-bureaucratic forms of organization", in Journal of Applied Behavioural Science, Vol. 13, 1977, No. 3.

[20] Gulowsen, J.: "A measure of work group anatomy" in Davis, L.E. and Taylor, J.: Design of jobs (Harmondsworth, Middx., Penguin, 1972).

THE DESIGN OF PRODUCTION SYSTEMS: NEW THINKING AND NEW LINES OF DEVELOPMENT

2

Rolf Lindholm and Sven Flykt*

1. Introduction

This chapter on the design of production systems covers approaches to setting up the production system from a purely technical point of view, the inclusion of the resources enabling the system to function, and the design of the work roles involved. The discussion will focus primarily on industrial processes, or those that closely resemble industrial processes in their general characteristics. However, these fundamental organisational principles are generally valid over a broad spectrum of activities, and should therefore be useful in non-manufacturing sectors as well.

As a starting-point for the discussion, we will look briefly at four criteria of a good production system: independence of small systems, a high degree of stability and resistance to production fluctuation, attractiveness of work roles and a good working environment. We believe that these points reflect the most important trends in modern production system design.

Thereafter, we will, with these basic points in mind, examine various approaches to production systems, with the aim of attaining over-all harmony between the basic principles and the systems that grow out of them.

Since we are not treating the entire subject in detail, but are focusing only on certain topics of current interest, we must emphasise one important limitation in our discussion: we are not presuming to show how any particular production system must be or should be

---

* Rolf Lindholm is President, The Swedish Management Group, Sven Flykt is with the Swedish Management Group.

41

designed.   We want only to demonstrate how some developments and approaches can be used.   Whether one or another of these is the most suitable solution in any particular case can only be determined in the light of all the special conditions surrounding the given situation.

2.   Criteria for production design

In the construction of a new factory or production system, the choice of specific design elements is always dictated by certain criteria of efficiency.   A high degree of machine utilisation, low labour costs, short throughput times, minimal materials waste, maximum flexibility - these are some of the terms in which efficiency goals are most commonly expressed.   A complete list of all aspects of a production system that might have a bearing on efficiency would, of course, be virtually endless.   For the purposes of the present discussion, we need not draw up an exhaustive list of these criteria, since our intention is to focus on only a limited number of elements.   Specifically, these are all related to:

- the place of the human being in the production system, and

- his interaction with technology.

It must be emphasised that our analysis will give special consideration to some particular working life factors - trends and current thinking regarding the labour market, production organisation and evolving attitudes toward work and the environment.   Against this background, we have identified four criteria that are of special significance in the design of production systems. The overriding principle from which they arise is that a factory should be an efficient production system and at the same time an attractive workplace for a human being. We have chosen to call these four criteria:

(i)   co-ordinated independence of small systems;

(ii)   a high degree of stability of the production system;

(iii)   task attractiveness;

(iv)   good working environment.

We will briefly comment on each of these criteria.

Co-ordinated independence of
small systems

By co-ordinated independence we mean a system formed by a network of production units of a moderate size, each of which can function independently. Dividing a production process into small independent units can be of great importance in simplifying administrative work. A decentralisation of this type is also a way of stimulating local initiatives. An organisation based on small independent units gives better opportunities of personal involvement and job satisfaction.

The extent to which a production process can be restructured into smaller independent units varies, of course, from case to case. In the attempts to divide large systems into smaller independent units there are four central issues:

- The actual possibilities of dividing a large system into several self-contained sections.

- The possibilities of organising smaller units around specific products or product groups in order to collect all the equipment needed for their complete manufacture within the unit.

- The degree of independence that can be achieved in a small unit, that is, the extent to which they can be self-contained with respect to various service functions, such as maintenance, material handling, etc.

- Finally, the method of arranging a "soft" over-all co-ordination and support of the small units.

High degree of stability

The ultimate judgement whether a production system adequately fulfils its objectives depends heavily on its degree of stability. The design of the production system has a profound influence on its stability, in terms both of limiting its sensitivity to fluctuations in the production system, and of maximising the ease with which planning and monitoring can be carried out. We will focus on three characteristics that can contribute to the stability of the system, namely:

- Simplified material-flow patterns are one important way of improving the degree of stability.

- Reliability and maintainability of production equipment and processes are of great significance in the
  achievement of production stability and a high rate
  of capacity utilisation.

- Work organisations and job design also affect the
  stability and reliability of a production system and
  its sensitivity to fluctuations in the production
  process and variations in the workforce. One
  example: if the production process can be divided
  into short, separate, parallel lines of production,
  the risks of major fluctuations are much lower than
  if the whole production process is carried out
  through one continuous line.

Attractiveness of jobs

Efforts to create more stimulating and satisfying
jobs are naturally related closely to trends in society
as a whole and to the higher level of expectation people
hold at present regarding their work. The attractiveness
of jobs is also of great importance from the point of
view of increasing workers' motivation, which in turn
affects the result obtained.

It is obvious that there are many factors at work
experienced by employees in their jobs, and that these
affect their job satisfaction. We will limit our discussions here to a few factors that are closely related
to the design of production systems:

- Well-designed production systems should include
  tasks with different degrees of difficulty.

- If work is to be stimulating and satisfying, it must
  provide a reasonable degree of autonomy for both
  individuals and groups.

- A production organisation based on groups and team
  work can be an effective way to enlarge and enrich
  jobs.

- The size of a production system should be such that
  workers can maintain both visual contact and social
  contact.

The physical working environment

The importance of a good physical working environment has been realised by many companies, which are
making extensive improvements in this area. The elimination of accident hazards and health risks is not the only

44

factor that is being considered, for the environment must
also be pleasant to work in. When new facilities are
being constructed, therefore, it is essential that they
form a place that is both safe to work in and sufficiently attractive, so that workers can be recruited easily
and, once hired, will want to stay.

The physical environment consists, of course, of
numerous factors, but we will focus on two inter-related
aspects, namely:

- The basic demand that <u>health and safety</u> risks must
  be minimised.

- A production environment that is <u>pleasant to work in
  for the workers</u>. This means a workplace of sufficient size and good layout and one that is well
  equipped with recreation facilities.

3. New principles for the grouping of production facilities

With the criteria discussed above as a basis for
designing a production system, our first step is to make
some over-all decisions on the grouping and placing of
production facilities.

Two main choices

In a process industry, such as steel or papermaking,
production generally depends on a single technological
unit in which all the inter-related pieces of equipment
combine to form one large "machine". There is virtually
no freedom of choice in grouping the machines or the
equipment used.

In lighter industry, on the other hand, the items
being manufactured usually go through several different
operations in different machines and at different work-
places. There are two main principles that may be
applied in grouping the equipment and sending materials
through the production system - functional grouping and
flow grouping - as shown in figure 1.

Functional grouping (operations layout)

In this alternative, all similar production equipment is located in its own organisational unit - a section or a department. A typical arrangement includes a
turning department, a welding department, a surface

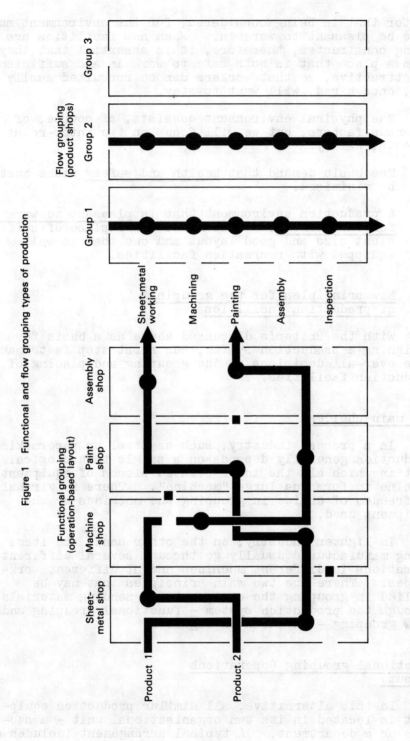

Figure 1 Functional and flow grouping types of production

treating department, and so on. Workers and supervisory personnel within each unit are specialists in the
type of operation for which they are responsible. If a
number of different products, each requiring its own distinct series of operations, are being manufactured, they
must be transported from department to department in the
order of the operations required.

Flow grouping (product shops)

In flow grouping, production equipment is placed in
a flow corresponding to the sequence of operations
required for the product. The organisational unit thus
becomes a chain of connected operations. Specialisation
is also present in this type of plant, but it is of a
different character. The supervisor and his co-workers
are primarily specialists in their product line.

Flow grouping gaining ground

The practice of grouping production equipment
according to the main flow-lines of production is becoming increasingly common, even in cases where the product
mix is quite varied. This can generate substantial
rationalisation benefits in terms of better resistance to
production fluctuations, a more efficient use of working
capital, and an opportunity to create more meaningful
jobs.

In a flow-grouped organisational unit, all the
necessary equipment for the entire chain of operations is
in a single supervisory area. The flow-group department
constitutes one planning point in the planning system.
Within the group, everyone can easily see the whole production process, jump in and take action when and where
breakdowns occur and share resources and personnel as
needed when delays or pile-ups take place.

Functional grouping requires careful planning and
control so that all products can travel in the correct
sequence of operations from department to department and
be completed on schedule. In practice, it is extremely
difficult to carry this work out satisfactorily. In
practice, in functionally grouped factories, there are
accumulations of materials and half-finished products
spread around in in-process inventories and buffer stock
at work stations. The throughput time tends to be long.

Flow grouping, on the other hand, cuts down on
materials handling and in-process materials inventories,
shortens throughput times and therefore reduces the cost
of working capital tied up in products moving through

the manufacturing process.   In addition, flow grouping
means that work organisation can be simpler and better.
Supervisors and workers span a portion of the production
process that contains many different tasks and makes
possible varied and enriched jobs.   This means that
workers have the opportunity to sharpen their skills and
learn additional jobs.   Moreover, it is easier to define,
keep track of and arrange feedback of meaningful results
and to create a unified responsibility for work results
in a supervisor and his co-workers.   This can induce
more involvement of the workers in their jobs.

Flow grouping at different levels

Flow grouping may be put into operation at various
levels in companies.   Small work groups can be organised
according to flow principles.   Similarly, it is possible
in many cases to organise a working area, a department or
an entire factory along the same lines.

The work group

A small work group can be organised for one sequence
of related operations.   By grouping the production
facilities in this sequence, we can create a simple working group for the product or group of products (see
figure 2).

It is not always possible in adopting a flow type of
production to ensure that operations in the flow will be
balanced.   This is especially true if the manufacturing
operation includes a number of different products.   In
some cases, however, this can be an advantage.   An im-
balance in manufacturing tasks means that workers must
switch tasks and help each other when the need arises,
which contributes to effective group work and provides
opportunities for the learning and broadening of jobs.

The supervisory area

A supervisory area can be designed so that it contains responsibility for one entire production line.
Ideally, the group should manufacture a complete product
under a single supervisor.   Let us look at a practical
example concerning a factory that manufactures certain
hygienic and medical products.   Originally, the plant
was conventionally organised according to the following
functions:

- materials inventories;

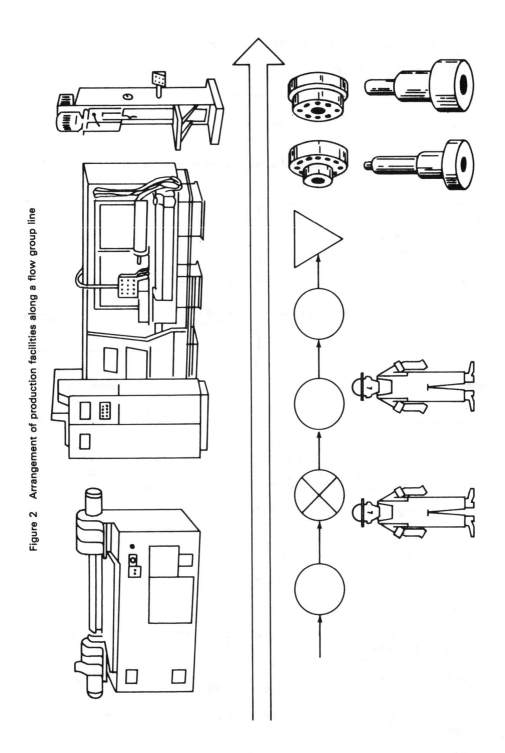

Figure 2 Arrangement of production facilities along a flow group line

- semi-fabricated manufacturing;

- manufacturing;

- finished goods inventories;

- maintenance (see figure 3).

Figure 3   The traditional layout of a medical products plant

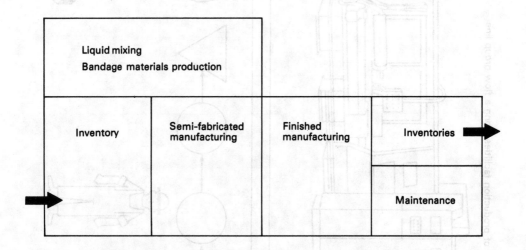

After the plant had been in operation for some time, the organisation was changed to a flow-based arrangement, divided into flow groups corresponding to:

- production of fruit salt;

- manufacture of sanitary cleansing devices for health use;

- production of cleansing towel;

- production of bandages (see figure 4).

The finished goods inventories and one other department remained as functional units.   This illustrates the fact that, in practice, it is not always possible to have complete functional grouping or complete flow grouping for all operations in a given plant.

In our example, the features of the new organisation are:

(1)   Each product group has its own supervisor.

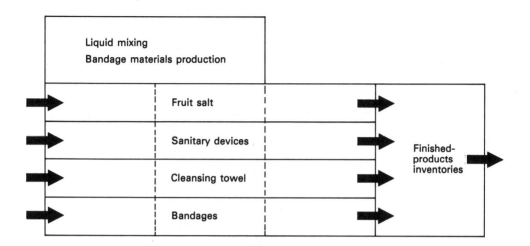

Figure 4   The new layout of a medical products plant

Liquid mixing
Bandage materials production

Fruit salt

Sanitary devices

Cleansing towel

Bandages

Finished-
products
inventories

(2)   Each group has its own maintenance and materials handling personnel.

(3)   Each supervisor may spend up to 2,000 kroner (about $400) at his own discretion, without clearance from his higher-ups.

(4)   No one from another department can request test runs, experiments or the like without "negotiating" with the supervisor on the timing and costs.

(5)   Each product group has its own materials inventory.

(6)   The supervisor has at his disposal a three-month over-all manning plan.   Apart from this basic framework, he is bound to no further directives for day-to-day operations, and makes all the necessary decisions himself.

(7)   Each product group has a clear responsibility for work performance, in respect of both quantity and quality.

(8)   Each product group receives continuous information on:

   -   productivity (production per man-hour),

   -   machine utilisation (times and capacities),

   -   raw materials consumption.

(9)   Each product group constitutes an economic profit centre with its own results-oriented budget (production, cash costs and internal transactions) worked out with the participation of the supervisor.

(10) The results-oriented budget is followed up on a monthly basis.

This new division of responsibilities has made it possible to analyse meaningful "business results" for each and every one of the work areas. This has in turn influenced the motivation and involvement of workers - and improved productivity as well.

The reorganisation from functional grouping to flow grouping in this case resulted in a 20 per cent increase in productivity over a three-year period, primarily because of faster action in correcting errors and more effective action in the placing of personnel.

To sum up, the advantages of a division into product groups instead of functional groups were the following in this case:

- more simplicity in defining and recording meaningful results;

- smoother delegation of responsibilities to supervisors and workers;

- increased flexibility and capacity to meet production fluctuations;

- enlarged jobs and more independence both for supervisors and for their associates;

- possibility of arranging "career planning" for workers;

- higher efficiency through:

    - shorter throughput times,

    - less capital tied up in in-process inventories,

    - increased productivity,

    - higher utilisation of capacity (through better resistance to breakdowns and disturbances).

Flow grouping at the factory level

Flow grouping can also be applied if the product itself is complicated, consisting of a number of related parts and components. In such a case, flow grouping is organised so that the constituent components are manufactored in a number of flow groups and thereafter assembled, possibly also with final testing in one or more further flow groups in the same factory. Responsibility for the finished product rests with a manager, but the advantages of flow groups are attained by using them as the organisational units within the factory, each of the flow groups being responsible for its portion of the finished product.

Again, the principle is best illustrated through a practical example. A factory for the manufacture of heat exchangers traditionally designed on a functional basis was transformed into a series of five flow groups, despite short series and a large number of product variations. The result was that throughput times and quantities of goods in process were substantially reduced. At the same time, an efficient organisation was created, built around team work. Figure 5 shows the layout of the factory.

The manager of the product line is now responsible for all the activities needed to manufacture the product. The necessary administrative functions are delegated to the production unit itself, and offices are located in the middle of the factory, grouping factory management, planning and resources for industrial engineering, and purchasing.

A guiding principle is the grouping of the entire production line from raw materials to finished product within the factory. This self-sufficiency is reinforced by the fact that the factory has its own resources for administration and service. There is very little dependence on other production units and the coordination of the product flow can be handled within the product shop. This means simplified planning and short throughput times for the products.

4. Independence of small systems

In our introductory remarks regarding criteria of good production systems, we noted that an effort should be made to give small units within a production system as much independence as possible. We will now discuss

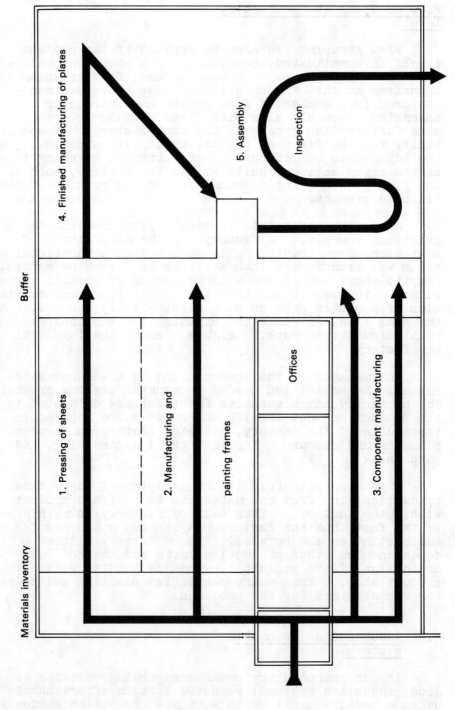

Figure 5   Layout of a heat exchanger factory

further measures that can be taken to bring about self-sufficiency in small systems.

The typical small company is an example of a self-sufficient production system on a small scale.   All decisions necessary for the unit's development and operation are taken within the company.   All resources needed for day-to-day operations are available, so that contacts with the outside world are limited.   The company has its own goals and own routines, so its progress can easily be followed.   Operations tend to be simple by dynamic and the work itself in a small company is often considered by employees to be more attractive than that in larger units.

Not all companies, factories and production systems, of course, are small.   Frequently, production systems must be large in order to attain sufficient volume for optimum operation and profitability.   But we should emphasise that, even in large production systems, efforts can often be advantageously made to design the systems so that they consist of smaller systems, each independent of the others.   Such independence in the smaller systems that make up a larger production unit can have many advantages, some of which we have already touched upon. Here we will discuss three types of measures that may be taken to increase the self-sufficiency of smaller units in a larger production system.   They are:

(1)   parallel lines of production flow;

(2)   buffers in the production flow;

(3)   a new form of production design that allows better division of work.

Parallelisation in the production flow

An increase in the capacity of an existing production unit can be achieved in two ways:

(1)   by increasing the capacity of the existing units;

(2)   by adding one or more parallel production units.

Let us look at a familiar example from industry. The moving line in the final assembly in an automobile factory is a single long inter-related chain of operations.   In order to increase production volume on this line, the speed can be increased.   If this is done, more workers must be added to achieve the higher assembly speed.   Consequently, each worker will have a shorter task cycle than before the production step-up.

In earlier times, this was in fact the most usual method of increasing production in systems of this type. But the approach has at least two substantial drawbacks:

(i) The system become increasingly sensitive to disturbances. If one operation in the line stops, all the other operations normally stop too. The high production capacity of the line means that large losses can be generated in a short period of time.

(ii) Work tasks become short, simple and rigidly fixed. In many cases, task time cycles are as low as one to two minutes. This can mean less interest on the part of the worker in his job, high personnel turnover and difficulty in maintaining the desired quality.

The establishment of parallel production flows has therefore become an increasingly common alternative to the large, single, inter-related flow. This means that the entire assembly, or at least a substantial part of the assembly, is done on several production lines mounted in parallel.

Figure 6 shows two systems that are identical in terms of production capacity. The work in both systems is performed at 12 work stations. In the line-grouped system, the work is divided into 12 operations. If the

Figure 6   Arrangement of production flow

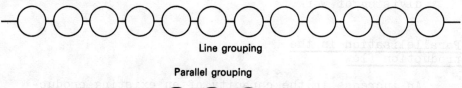

Line grouping

Parallel grouping

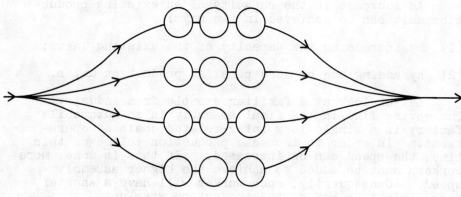

flow is mechanically controlled (which is not unusual), the work done at all stations must require the same amount of time - otherwise, waiting times will occur (so-called balancing losses). In the parallel-grouped system, the work is done in several parallel flows, with a smaller number of stations in each flow.

The advantages of parallel grouping are:

- Production reliability. If one station breaks down, only a small part of the total production system is affected.

- Ease of introducing product variations. In parallel systems, it is easier to deal with product variations. For example, two-door cars can be assembled in one group, four-door cars in another group, right-hand drive cars in a third, and so on.

- Better job content and work organisation. Opportunities are greater for creating work with a richer content. There are also greater opportunities for production group members to bear the responsibility for their own work and for its quality.

- Expansion flexibility. The system can be expanded step by step through the addition of more parallel flow groups. Such expansions can often be carried out without disturbing other parts of the production system.

- Clearer responsibility for results. The reporting of various kinds of results is facilitated - for example, the measurement of productivity for each group. Because it is relatively easy to keep track of products as they move through the system, the skills and quality reflected in each product can be traced back to a product group. This tends to increase the interest among workers in achieving good-quality results.

- Varying manning possibilities. Capacity can be varied when demand varies, through manning more or fewer of the parallel units. The rebalancing that would be necessary in complete line grouping is not needed here.

Let us look at a practical example. A shop for the assembly of engines (at Saab-Scania), put into operation in 1972, was the first large-scale example in the automobile industry of the elimination of the assembly line and its replacement by several parallel subsystems. The arrangement has worked well, and this basic idea has inspired many imitators within the European motor

industry and in other fields.   The assembly of the
engine, which requires approximately 30 minutes, is done
by small groups working in parallel loops (see figure 7).
There are seven such loops, of which five are regularly
used.   The sixth is used for training purposes, and the
seventh can be put into operation when production capacity has to be increased.

In this system, parallel grouping has been used to
good advantage.   The groups can work at different speeds
without upsetting the over-all flow.   The normal manning
level is three operators per loop, but the work can proceed even if two of the three are absent.   At times when
considerable capacity increases are needed, up to six
operators can be assigned to each loop.   Moreover, the
number of loops in operation can easily be varied.

Let us look at another example of parallel flows
from the motor industry.   This is the Saab-Scania body
factory at Trollhättan in Sweden, where, in order to
achieve advantages similar to those mentioned above, an
inter-related production system with numerous work stations in a chain has been replaced by a series of
parallel work groups, each of which carries out the
entire sequence of tasks on the body.   The work consists
primarily in welding and grinding.   The introduction of
the new system means that all the tasks needed to complete the work on already assembled bodies are performed
at each of about 20 stations.   At each station there are
two workers who work together.   It takes 45 to 60 minutes for them to finish the job, depending on the model.
In the old arrangement, incorporating a fixed-speed
assembly line, the task cycles were 3 minutes per working
station.

As regards work organisation, the parallel stations
have been organised in production teams or production
groups.   Each group consists of 6 ordinary group
members, of whome six work at one of the three stations
(see figure 8).   The seventh member is the contact man
for the group and handles indirect jobs integrated in the
group's total responsibility - for example, quality control.   This role rotates among the members on a weekly
basis.   Figure 8 also shows that the bodies pass a
quality control point after leaving the area of the group.
If necessary, the bodies can be returned for adjustment
to the particular group responsible for the fault.

In this project, the following advantages have been
achieved with the help of parallel grouping:

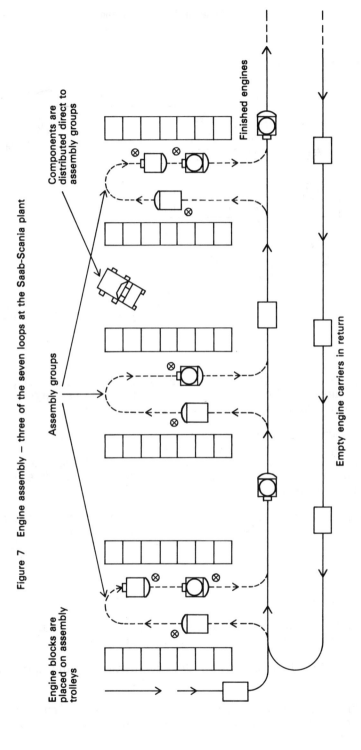

Figure 7 Engine assembly – three of the seven loops at the Saab-Scania plant

Engine blocks are placed on assembly trolleys

Assembly groups

Components are distributed direct to assembly groups

Finished engines

Empty engine carriers in return

59

Figure 8   Three of the parallel stations

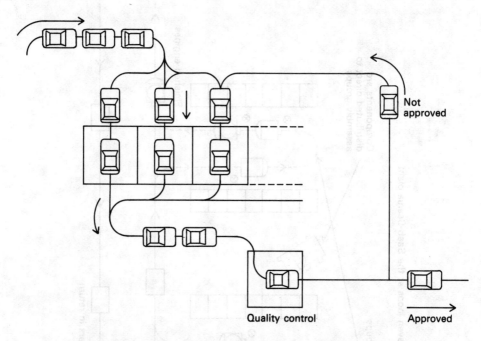

- jobs with natural borders have been created; one
  stage in the manufacture of bodies is begun and
  completed at a single work station;

- production groups have been formed with complete
  responsibility for production, including the quality
  of their own work, plus auxiliary tasks such as
  materials requisitions, maintenance of their own
  equipment, etc.

Capital investment costs for the changeover - about
10 million kroner ($2 million) - were amortised in less
than three years.   The greatest advantages of the new
system from the industrial engineering and financial
viewpoints, have been:

- greater production reliability;

- reduced needs for personnel, in great part because
  of the elimination of balancing losses;

- a reduction of costs for adjustment and quality
  control of about 20 per cent;

- the capacity of the system to undergo substantial
  changes in production volume without new balancing
  procedures.

Buffers in the production flow

It is often deemed desirable to increase the autonomy of a small system forming part of a larger unit, with respect to its immediate working environment. In such cases, some sort of buffer stock arrangement must be provided before and after the unit in the over-all system. Different units in the production flow do not produce exactly the same volume in each production cycle, but tend to vary constantly. If a certain production unit is to avoid having to function on a "hand-to-mouth" basis with respect to the immediately preceding unit, there must be a buffer stock of materials on which work can commence whenever the unit is ready. In turn, there must be another buffer stock after that unit and before the subsequent stage in the production chain.

In most types of production, a certain buffer stock normally builds up between different production groups. In this way, each individual group can function independently of its immediate working environment.

There are, however, important exceptions to this rule. We will therefore look at the problem of self-sufficiency in small systems in such cases. We will again choose an example from the motor industry, this time from Volvo. Volvo's well-known Kalmar factory is the world's first motor plant where final assembly is done without a fixed-speed assembly line. One of the problems that was solved with this innovation was the creation of greater independence, with respect to preceding and following groups, for small units (production groups, assembly teams) within the larger system. This could be done because the new technology facilitated the use of buffers in the production flow. It was done as follows.

Each basic car body is transported from work team to work team on a self-steering trolley guided by electric tracks embedded in the floor. These trolleys move automatically between the teams and stop in parking places provided for this purpose before and after the groups (see figure 9). There is room for three trolleys in each space between teams, constituting the assembly team's buffers. These buffers make it easier, in comparison with a conventional system, for the workers to work at their own pace, to take breaks, to handle unforeseen breakdowns and so on. The factory's new technology, incorporating buffers, has considerably increased the autonomy of these small units. The spreading of disturbances throughout the line occurs much less often here than in a conventional arrangement.

Figure 9   Incoming and outgoing buffer at Volvo's Kalmar plant

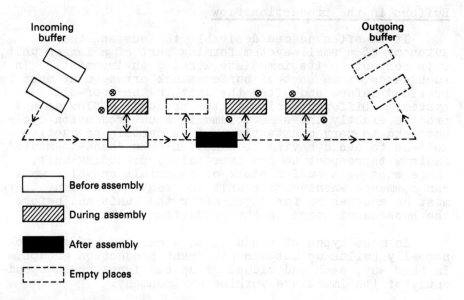

Incoming buffer

Outgoing buffer

☐ Before assembly

▨ During assembly

■ After assembly

▭ Empty places

Changed product design for better systems division

Sometimes it is not possible to chop up a large production system into independently functioning small morsels.   In the case of a complex product that must be put together step by step in one long process, the production system cannot be easily cut into smaller segments.   A typical example is the assembly of a large and complicated product, such as an automobile, a TV set, or a complex household appliance.   Often, this assembly must be done in one coherent process because the different components are closely interconnected in such a way that it is difficult to divide them into smaller chunks. In such a case, the production system can be designed in only one way - one continuing process with one production flow.   It is difficult to bring about any reasonable independence in the smaller systems that make up the over-all unit.   The risk of spreading breakdowns from one point in the flow to other points is great, and the work in this type of system is less attractive to the worker.

However, in these cases it is often possible to change the product design so that the production process can in fact be broken up into smaller units.   If the product can be designed so that it is systematically constructed of modules or building blocks that can be manufactured separately, and then put together in a final assembly operation, it becomes possible to create the necessary conditions for a production system composed of small independent systems. This method of building up complex products in the form of systematic module arrangements has become increasingly common in many production operations.

Let us look at another practical example. This one comes from the Huskvarna Company in Sweden, which manufactures numerous products, including electric cookers. This type of production was previously carried out only along assembly lines similar to those of traditional motor plans, that is, long assembly lines where a conveyor belt ran through a materials inventory and where the various components were picked up and put together at the different work stations. Jobs consisted in short time cycles and rigidly prescribed routines.

The company wanted to reshape the production system so that it could take the form of a group of independently functioning, smaller systems. But in order to achieve this, it was found that the product itself had to be changed. A new cooker model was therefore developed, consisting of seven modules or building blocks (see figure 10). Each of these was manufactured in an independent unit in the company and they were all put together in the final assembly.

The system had the following characteristics:

(i)   each module can be produced in a shielded, independent production unit;

(ii) the modules are designed for production in short chains of operations;

(iii) the modules have their own functions that can be tested and adjusted in their respective production units.

5.   Line-oriented transport
     and handling systems

Following our discussion of the over-all issue of grouping production facilities and thereby focusing attention on flow-orientation and the independence of small systems, we now arrive at another important problem area, that of transport and handling systems. In many types of industrial production, there are massive quantities of materials that must be regularly and continually picked up and moved through the production system. In certain types of production involving especially large volumes of materials, the materials-handling system has

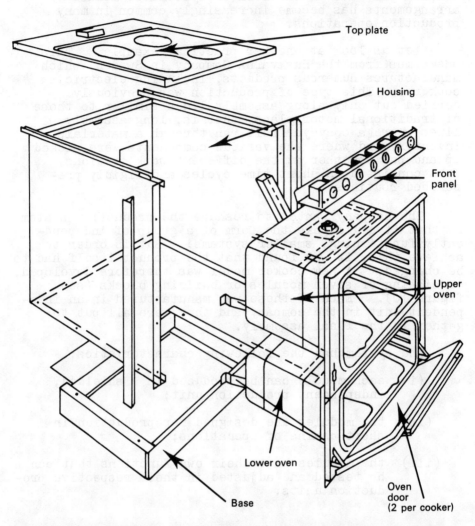

Figure 10 Changing product design to allow production in smaller groups

Top plate

Housing

Front panel

Upper oven

Lower oven

Base

Oven door (2 per cooker)

overshadowed other questions and the materials-handling issue has come to be the determining factor in the design of the over-all system.   The final assembly of auto-mobiles, under the traditional system, is a good example of this.   The mechanically powered conveyor belt that travels through the factory (that is, the materials inven-tory) has shaped the basic structure of this kind of pro-duction system.   In fact, it was impossible to depart from this type of work organisation before new solutions had been found for the handling problems.

In this section, we will examine the handling equip-ment that is best adapted to the kind of production arrangement we have been emphasising.   In view of our stress on flow orientation and product groups, it is of interest to discuss the so-called line-oriented handling systems, that is, systems that can move materials along given flow lines.

Factors affecting the choice of materials-handling equipment

When, in an individual case, it is necessary to find a suitable solution to a materials handling problem, there is a long string of factors that must be analysed. The most important are as follows:

Direction of materials flow. The main alternatives are:

- straight-line flow (this is the simplest type, comprising one starting point, one finishing point and one direction of movement);

- diverging/converging flow (this is used in certain cases, for example, parallel production lines);

- return flow (this takes place, for example, when defective work is sent back for correction. It also takes place when a product must pass one station twice);

- detour possibilities (it may be necessary to provide detour facilities for fast materials flow through a production unit, for example, when certain products are not worked at all work stations or are worked upon only to differing degrees).

The product. The qualities of the product or of the material that is to be handled generally have the greatest influence on the choice of transport equipment. The most important qualities of the product that affect the choice are:

- size,

- weight,

- shape,

- fragility,

- consistency.

It is also important to note that the transport system must often handle more than one product or product variant. Moreover, during the production process the product might change its characteristics, and this has to be taken into consideration.

Frequency of movement. The design of a system for maximum transport frequency is expensive and results in a poor degree of utilisation of the materials-handling equipment. The dimensions are therefore placed somewhere between average and maximum values. The goal is to optimise waiting times and capacity utilisation at the same time.

Varying production speed. A certain freedom within a work group means that varying production speeds will be experienced in different operations.

Materials-handling equipment as an auxiliary to work station operations. The materials-handling system should be designed so that handling at the work stations is as efficient as possible. This system is sometimes used both as a means of movement and as an architectual fixture defining the area belonging to a particular work organisation.

Manoeuvrability. If products are to be transported to different work stations, information must be made available on which products are to be so routed, and on their destinations. This requires:

- despatching ability: the system must enable products to be sent to different work stations;

- identification: practicability of giving each product an identity so that its movements can be traced later;

- changes of priorities: the system must offer the possibility of changing the order of handling if an "express order" must have priority.

Flexibility. This is the capacity of the handling system to allow changes in the materials flow over a longer or shorter time. For example:

- product variations;

- defective products;

- rearrangement of production premises.

(As an example of flexibility in handling systems, we can mention "loop-guided" equipment. This allows the rearrangement of materials-handling lines in a production area with a minimum of bother. A loop can easily be made inactive, and new loops can easily be embedded in

the production system (say the plant floor) when new
routes are needed.)

Possibilities of mechanisation. In the past,
mechanisation has been primarily applied to processing
done at work stations, but more recently the same
interest has been increasingly devoted to transport and
handling operations. This has happened primarily because of the need to minimise working capital tied up in
in-process inventories. Below are some other factors
that may influence a decision to mechanise handling:

- large materials flow;

- large volume of materials;

- high weight of materials;

- long transport distances;

- complex flow patterns;

- high speed of movement.

Technical demands on the handling system. Examples:

- operational reliability;

- environmental effects (sound level, health and accident risks for personnel);

- ease of maintenance (accessibility, replacement
  component availability, etc.);

- resistance to environment.

Transport and handling systems. In a product shop
or a flow group, the balancing of production capacities
for all operations is not a primary goal. In order to
even out variations and at the same time use available
capacity efficiently, it is sometimes necessary to use
buffer stock. In many cases it is desirable that the
transport and handling system be able to fulfil that
demand as well.

Some examples of transport equipment

Below is a brief description of some five groups of
transport equipment that may be worth considering in the
type of work organisation we have been discussing. This
cavalcade of different technical solutions is primarily

intended to impart some ideas regarding the solution
sought in designing new forms of work organisation.

(i) Conveyors:

Roller conveyors. Roller conveyors are a common
form of the line-oriented transport of goods on a pallet
or other type of material with a flat underside.   In
level transport, no motors or other drive mechanisms are
needed.   They can be combined with auxiliary devices
such as axles and elevators.   Roller conveyors in their
simplest form are a cheap, flexible and virtually
maintenance-free means of transport.

Wheel conveyors. The wheel path is generally made
up of supporting beams similar to those used in lighter
roller conveyors.   Instead of rollers, there are axles
with wheels.   They are either placed in a line, one
after the other, or in a zigzag fashion.   Goods transported on wheel conveyors must be relatively solid, with
a flat surface and not too heavy.   They are cheaper than
roller conveyors, and they are therefore especially
appropriate for the transport of goods with large volume
in relation to their weight.

Conveyor belts. This class of conveyor belt
includes all the devices whose transport capacities consist essentially in an endless belt on which material is
transported.   A transport belt can be of rubber, cloth,
leather, steel or some other material.   The belt runs
along a series of rollers, or slides on a fixed foundation.   With respect to materials, conveyor belts can be
divided into three basic groups:

- belt conveyors;

- steel strip transport;

- web conveyors.

The appropriate material is selected with reference to
the character of the materials to be transported and
other environmental factors.

Chain conveyors (figure 11(a)). A chain conveyor
consists of one or more chains running along a support
between drive wheels and freely turning wheels.   Chain
conveyors are used for transporting materials over long
distances (up to 300 metres), where roller conveyors are
not feasible.   They are also especially useful in transporting very wide products, such as sheet metal plates.

Slat conveyors (figure 11(b)).   A slat conveyor is
essentially made up of two chain conveyors with the product placed on slats fixed between the two chains.   Each
slat is fastened to a chain at each end.   Each link in
the chain incorporates a carrying wheel that moves on
rails or in a metal guidance track.   The slats are made
of steel or wood, depending on the particular application.
There are two basic types of slats - "overlapping" and
"non-overlapping".   Slat conveyors are especially suitable for heavy and awkward products.   Carrying capacities can run as high as 1,000 tons per hour.

Table conveyors (figure 11(c)).   These tables
rotate continuously, and are often combined with automatic loading and unloading stations.   When an operator
finishes his work on a product, he can address it to
another operator at another work station.   If the
unloading table is full, the product makes another turn
round the conveyor and is unloaded the next time there is
a place free at the station.   The conveyor can serve as
an addressing device, transport and buffer.

(ii)   Overhead conveyors:

Circular conveyors (figure 11(d)).   As the name
implies, a circular conveyor carries materials round in a
fixed cycle during manufacturing.   If not unloaded, the
materials will return to the starting point on the conveyor.   Normally, however, they are loaded and unloaded
several times during the cycle.   The circular conveyor
is one of the most useful types of conveyors in that it
is, unlike most varieties, three-dimensional.   It permits transport in straight or curved lines and both
horizontally and vertically.   It offers endless possibilities of combinations of movements and can be short or
long - some are several kilometres in length.   Circular
conveyors can also be combined with storage racks and
other circular conveyors.   This type of conveyor is
extremely flexible regarding both length and design.

A circular conveyor in its simplest form can be
found in the ready-made clothing industry, where hangers
carrying cloth are transported through the manufacturing
process on rods.   In other applications, we find moving
trolleys, which are fixed at regular intervals in a
closed circle, running along a metal beam.   Indeed, a
circular transport conveyor system can transport virtually any kind of material in passing through innumerable
manufacturing operations.   The materials can be large or
small, heavy or light.   Materials of different size and
weight can be handled at the same time on the same transport system, and they can be carried hot or cold and
through a variety of processes such as cleaning,

painting, drying and blasting.   Such a system can be
used simultaneously as both a transport system and as an
in-process inventory between manufacturing processes.

Chain-powered trolley (figure 11(e)).   In many
shops there are transport systems equipped with hand-
powered trolleys.   If the transport system is straight
and one-way, it can often be economic to couple the
trolleys to a chain along the flow path.   The chain runs
in a metal track that lies either above the floor or sunk
in it.   The trolleys can also be powered by an overhead
system attached to the roof.

Overhead circular conveyors with individually guided
trolleys.   In this type of circular system, trolleys are

installed at Saab-Scania in Trollhättan and ASG in Malmö,
Sweden.   In the ASG installation each electrical trolley
is equipped with a switchbox containing three dials.   The
dials are set to match the code number of a particular
station and the rest follows automatically.   A trolley
starts from its spur and moves towards the main track.
If the main track is free, a switch is automatically
thrown and the trolley proceeds to the track.   When the
trolley approaches the spur that corresponds to the pre-
set number code, another switch is automatically thrown,
and the trolley slides into the spur and stops.   The
entire installation is equipped with a control system
that prevents the trolleys and their loads from touching
each other.

(iii)   Hoists:

The hoist consists of a cylinder with grooves for a
cable combined with a driving motor and brake in one unit.
It is fitted out with apertures and connections that permit it to be fixed in various ways, either stationary or
on transport trolleys.

Numerous different types of cranes and winches can
easily be constructed with the help of hoists.   Some
smaller types of hoists are equipped with rollers or
chains instead of cables.   The lifting capacity is
usually one-quarter of a ton, one-half of a ton, or one
ton, and such hoists are ideal for inserting a piece of
metal into a machine tool for working.   In some models
there is a gear device permitting the precise adjustment
of height for fastening in the chuck.   For special purposes - for example, in environments that are particularly dirty or where there is a danger of explosion, or

70

Figure 11   Some of the transport devices described in the text – a: Accumulating chain conveyor, b: Slat conveyor, c: Table conveyor, d: Circular conveyor, e: Chain-driven trolleys, f: Schematic sketch of air cushion

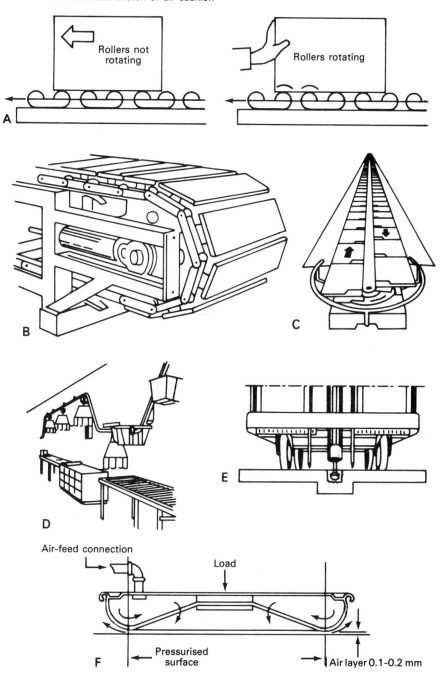

where a portable installation is desired - there are
hoists driven by fork-lift trucks.

(iv) <u>Driverless fork-lift trucks</u>:

A driverless fork-lift truck with wagons attached
can be programmed to follow precise paths in a factory.
There are two main ways in which automatic guidance can
be ensured:

(1) the truck can be guided by a guidance wire, running
     in a depressed floor track;

(2) the truck can be guided without mechanical contact
     with the environment:

     - by a magnetic field emanating from a cable
       embedded in the floor,

     - by photocells triggered by a luminous tape
       affixed to the floor.

(v) <u>Vertical transport and
     handling systems</u>:

<u>Chutes</u>. A chute consists of a shaped slide of metal
or other materials angled so that the materials slide
along the path.   A chute is a simple device for moving
materials between work stations or from a higher storage
area among other purposes.

<u>Lifting tables</u>. A simple lifting table can connect
two or more transport levels.   The load area can be
designed as a powered roller conveyor or an ordinary conveyor belt.

<u>Lifts</u>.   Where transport is sporadic and used with
low to medium frequency, a lift may be suitable, since it
operates between different levels and in both directions.

<u>Transport and handling systems
used as buffers</u>

(i) <u>Carrying conveyors</u>:

<u>Chain conveyors (figure 11(a))</u>.   The accumulation
of goods on a chain transport system obeys the same
principles as that on a roller conveyor.   Materials rest
on the rollers, placed either between the chain parts or
direct on the chains.   When the material is being

transported, the rollers do not rotate, and the materials move at the speed of the chains. When materials accumulate, they stop while the chains continue to turn, and the rollers rotate under the materials. The underside of the materials being moved should be flat.

Roller conveyors. If in a slat conveyor we replace the slats with rollers, we have an accumulation conveyor. When materials are blocked, the carrying rollers rotate against the underside of the materials while the conveyor belt beneath continues to run. This is especially suitable for heavy materials.

(ii) Overhead conveyors:

"Power-and-free" conveyors. A continuously powered chain runs in a guide rail. Under this rail there is another guide rail or a metal beam carrying non-powered trolleys in which load carriers are hanging. Under the chain there are hooks coupling the trolleys to the chain. The coupling is easily disconnected, so that the trolleys can be switched over to another branch of the system when required. The coupling is also disconnected when trolleys come into contact with each other.

Stan-run. The principle of this system is the same as that of roller conveyors. The trolleys hang above the rollers of the powered chain via a horizontal plate. If the trolley stops, the chain rollers slide past the trolley.

(iii) Floor-level conveyors:

Chain-powered trolleys (figure 11(e)). Accumulation can occur on the same principles as those governing overhead conveyors.

Driverless fork-lift trucks. Automatic loop-guided trolleys permit variations in production speeds because the trolleys can stand in line between production stages. The loops cost little and can easily be moved. In this way, accumulating trolleys can be placed in appropriate spots or in separate buffer loops when the production speed or the product programme is changed.

6. Decentralised production services

So far, we have highlighted developments that imply decentralisation and increased independence in small systems. If a smaller unit, such as a product shop, is to attain a high degree of autonomy with respect to its environment, it must possess its own defined tasks and its own appropriate resources for day-to-day production. We will now consider some of the ways in which such decentralised production services can be established, examining three examples of production functions that can be decentralised. These are production planning, quality control and maintenance and repair.

It may be recalled, however, that we began this discussion by referring to the development of the over-all organisation of companies and we will first return briefly to this point.

Organisation plans - yesterday and today

In past periods of industrial development, most companies had an organisation clearly divided by function: production, sales, finance, personnel, and so on. Within each of these main functions there were further divisions into subfunctions, following the same principles. An organisational chart for the production function within a company was often something like that shown in figure 12. In more recent years, however, most companies have changed their organisational design for a more product-oriented structure, where each production unit has a unified responsibility for all the functions needed to manufacture a certain product. This product orientation was first put into operation at top management levels, but different product units with entire responsibility for products within a given section of the product line evolved later to apply the same principles at lower hierarchical levels. Today, therefore, a company's organisational pattern often resembles that shown in figure 13.

One consequence of this trend in organisation structure has been that the function of central staff in large companies has been broken up and divided among the various product divisions and product units. Each product unit must therefore carry the entire responsibility for its production operation, and have at its disposal sufficient resources for staff functions such as planning, control or repairs.

Earlier in our discussion, we recommended that this organisational structure should be applied all the way down to the shop floor. Giving effect in this way to a product-divided, integrated form of work organisation implies that different production services can be decentralised to small units such as product shops.

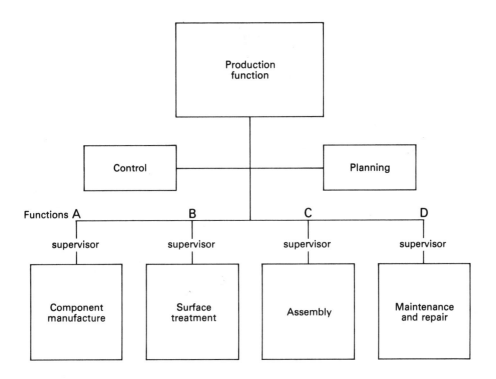

Figure 12 Organisation of production activities by function

Production planning

    In a product shop responsible for the manufacture of
a complete product or a complex product component on a
self-sufficient basis, day-to-day production planning
must be done within the shop in the immediate vicinity of
the flow lines where the product is made. The flow
orientation that we discussed in an earlier section
naturally leads to a dramatic simplification of the planning process compared with the more conventional functional organisation. Nevertheless, there must be constant feedback of what is happening on the production
lines to make alterations possible and to take corrective
action when needed.

    So that these tasks may be carried out in the pro-
duct shop, a choice must be made among an endless variety
of arrangements to suit the needs of the particular
organisation. In a small product shop, production planning responsibility might be only one of the tasks of a
white-collar employee, one of the small staff of persons
that must be placed within each product shop area. In
a somewhat larger product shop, one or more persons
might have production planning for sole responsibility.

Figure 13   Organisation of production activities by process

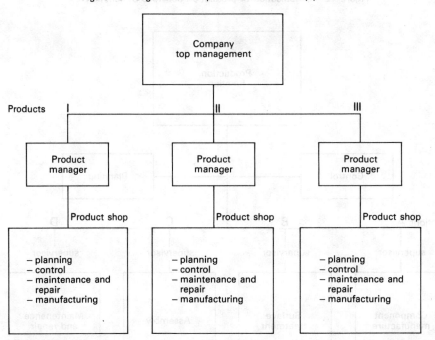

Since day-to-day production planning takes place
within the product shop, in the same area as the manufacturing, it is possible for supervisors and workers
within the unit to be involved in planning questions and
to participate actively in taking measures to attack problems when they first begin to appear.

More often, this type of product shop forms part of
a larger production system - the entire company or one
division of the company with its own characteristics.
The product that a product shop manufactures may be a
component of a larger assembled product.   Therefore,
there must usually be an over-all planning system within
which the product shop operates and whose general objectives it must meet.   Sales come in from the sales department;   over-all manning plans and delivery requirements
from other departments;   all purchasing might be done in
one centralised unit.   But even if the work in the product shop is determined by outside forces, such as orders
from the higher levels of the larger system, it is nevertheless important to have as much decentralisation as
possible so that day-to-day planning problems can be
worked out at the level where knowledge of these problems
exists.   Such decentralisation also makes it possible
for the persons who work within a unit to participate in
the planning activity.

Quality control

An effort to decentralise as much as possible should also be made in the quality control function. If a unit has sole responsibility for manufacturing a certain product or product component from beginning to end, it is also vital that the task of checking and meeting existing quality requirements be included in the unit along with other duties.

If this type of arrangement is to be established, the independent unit - a product shop, for example - must be given its own resources and its own organised routines, adequate to an active and careful handling of quality questions. These tasks can be the responsibility of a supervisor, or of persons who are especially selected to devote themselves entirely to quality. In any case, here too we find that locating the activity near the production operation, where quality problems arise, creates an opportunity for everyone involved in the production process to be involved in the control of quality as well - so that we have active participation from those who create the quality ... or the quality problems. It is essential, however, for the desired quality to be defined in such a way as to clarify ideas on both good quality and poor quality and made known to the working group.

Another requirement is an efficient system of day-to-day recording of quality results. This record-keeping must be done at frequent intervals and immediate feedback must be given to the place in the production process where errors have occurred. The primary aim must be to discover errors quickly enough for the necessary adjustments to be made before substantial damage is done.

Maintenance and repair

Our third example of a production function is that of maintenance and repair. This is also a field where extensive decentralisation is in harmony with the type of production system that we have been discussing. Let us look at two approaches that have frequently been followed with good results:

(1) The operator of a machine can be given the job of carrying out preventive maintenance on the machine and doing some simple repairs.

(2) Specialists in maintenance and repair can be included in the personnel of the production group or product shop.

Such measures produce a high degree of integration of production and maintenance resources within the product shop, so that corrective action may be taken with the necessary resources when something goes wrong. It is quite simple to have certain smaller equipment easily accessible, and for those who work on a day-to-day basis with certain production equipment to acquire a basic knowledge of its characteristics. Workloads for local repair personnel can be evened out through preventive measures and the involvement of these workers to some extent in direct production.

In large companies with complicated technology, however, it is obviously impossible to decentralise all maintenance work all the way down to the level of a product shop or production group. There are three principal factors that limit the degree of decentralisation:

(i) The need for specialised knowledge is of great importance in limiting decentralisation. Within small organisational units, it is not possible to use highly specialised experts efficiently. Such persons must be organised on a centralised basis or be brought in from outside the company to work as consultants.

(ii) The use of expensive specialised equipment also limits opportunities of a given unit for handling all the maintenance work that may be necessary. For example, if a certain maintenance routine that is carried out at infrequent intervals calls for the use of complex and expensive electronic measurement devices, and such equipment is also required for other jobs in a large company, it is quite natural for the equipment to be kept under the control of a centralised maintenance department.

(iii) Personnel requirements for major maintenance tasks vary widely over time. It is not possible for a small unit to possess sufficient resources to handle major breakdowns.

Thus efforts should be made to decentralise maintenance and repair functions as much as possible to groups and product shops. But, as indicated above, there are limits to the process of decentralisation.

7. Attractive jobs in a good
   working environment

In this concluding section, we will discuss how individual work roles in our production system can be

78

adapted to the people who are to work in it, and how the working environment can be made safe and attractive.

Interesting and stimulating
work roles

In earlier sections, we have discussed many of the conditions that determine the character of an individual's job in the production system. As will be clear from the discussion, our purpose has largely been to create production systems that are both efficient and pleasant to work in. This can be done by applying the over-all principles that we have been examining.

Let us now turn to some of the criteria and judgements that may be relevant when individual work stations and work roles are being shaped in the project planning stage in accordance with the basic point of view we have been taking. We will set forth this discussion under a number of "rules of thumb" that can serve as subtopics.

Avoid excessively short and
monotonous task cycles

Short task cycles can be advantageous in that they require short learning times. But a job that takes only a minute to do and must be repeated 500 times a day can very soon become monotonous. In fact it is not necessary to carry specialisation so far for the sake of production efficiency. There have been numerous approaches in recent years to transforming short-cycle jobs, and by now there is an abundance of experimental evidence showing that there is no real need to reduce cycle times to one minute and that they can in many cases be stretched to 10 or 15 minutes without any sacrifice in efficiency. The advantages of simpler forms of work organisation and less monotonous work easily offset the disadvantages of a lower degree of specialisation.

Avoid jobs that require a rigid
connection between man and machine

To be rigidly bound to a certain machine, to perform a fixed, limited set of gestures, to push certain buttons in a prescribed order - this kind of work can be excessively boring and cause considerable stress for the individual. Moreover, it is not a good solution from the point of view of production efficiency, since the operation comes to a halt as soon as the individual worker interrupts the routine of movements.

In the past few years, we have seen innumerable efforts to loosen the man-machine connection in short-cycle operations. The objective has been partly to humanise work and partly to increase the efficiency of production equipment. Let us illustrate this point with an example.

The placing of a piece of work in a precise position in a machine tool is often difficult to automate. Under the conventional method the operator sets up the piece direct on the machine table, that is, first removes the previous component and then inserts the new one in the same place (figure 14).

Figure 14   Machine/operator dependability

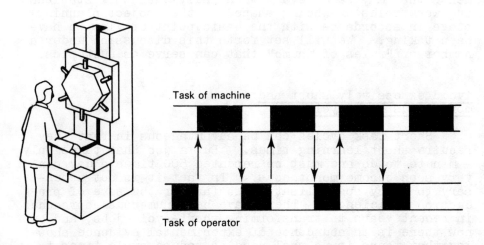

Task of machine

Task of operator

The operator's job is rigidly controlled by the machine and alternates between passive supervision and intense periods of work. The use of magazines loaded with components and automatic feeding can free the operator from the machine connection, even for longer periods (figure 15).

The next step is to connect several different machines together with automatic transport systems (figure 16). In this way, a component can pass several work stations with no need for the intervention of an operator.

Breaking the man-machine link offers several advantages:

- the operator can use his working time more freely and take a rest period when he or she wants;

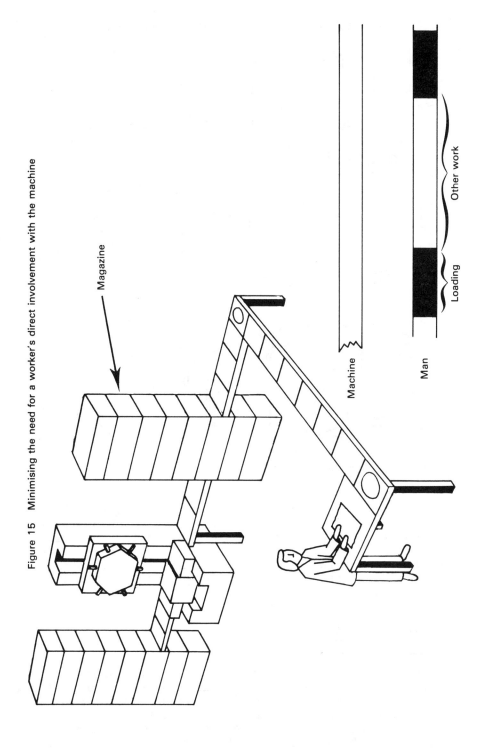

Figure 15   Minimising the need for a worker's direct involvement with the machine

81

Figure 16   Decreasing further worker's involvement through automation

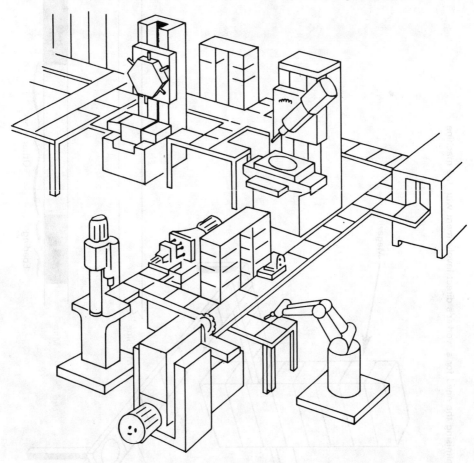

- several different tasks can be combined to form a number of stages in manufacturing, which means an enlarged work area and more variety for the worker;

- the stress that sometimes results from movements timed to precise machine operations can be eliminated.

Jobs in work teams to create contact and variety

We have been discussing the over-all characteristics of the production system, which include flow orientation, decentralisation and self-sufficient production groups. But it is essential to add other requirements to this basic set, and first and foremost that of shaping the work organisation to facilitate team work, spontaneous co-operation between workers in different jobs and

82

independent initiatives from individuals and groups in day-to-day work. If this general direction is followed, the work organisation can handle everyday problems and disturbances and attain good production results without any complicated administration of details.

Such a form of work organisation can thus be good for the enterprise. It can also be good for the individual. A team offers contact with the other members and a feeling of cohesiveness. There are opportunities to try various tasks within the province of the team and therefore to change jobs, learn more skills and develop personally and professionally. It should not be necessary to remain tied to a single job indefinitely. Moreover, team work shows the members how each job contributes to the end result, and they can therefore better understand the context of the larger operation in which they take part.

A safe and attractive working environment

This subject is so extensive and has so many ramifications that it should have an entire book to itself. But the creation of a good working environment is an integral part of the design of a production system, and we must therefore, in discussing the latter, touch on certain aspects of the physical environment. We will limit our discussion of this subject to two main topics that have a particular importance for production system design. Beyond that, readers are referred to the rich literature specifically devoted to environmental issues. The two important topics we will treat here are: (1) the occupational health risks that can arise from chemicals and other materials used in the production process, and (2) the possible influence that the design of the building sheltering our production system can have in reinforcing the type of organisation that we have been advocating.

New chemical risks

Much work has been done recently on improving the physical environment of various forms of work organisations. Considerable efforts have been made in the suppression of noise, the reduction of air pollution and the control of temperature through better ventilation systems, etc. One problem that has assumed ever-increasing importance is that of chemical health risks. Each year, approximately 1,000 new substances are put on the market. Some that are particularly important in industry are the following:

- new types of plastics;

- lubricating oil additives;

- new solvents;

- new adhesives.

The problem is partly to discover when new materials present a health risk, and partly, when this is known, to eliminate the risk from the production process.

Let us look at one example selected from the discussions of environmental problems in recent years - polyvinyl chloride (PVC). Since the alarming reports of the effects of PVC on the human body were published in 1974, the development in one Swedish factory producing this material was as shown in figure 17.

Figure 17 PVC-quantities in factory premises at different measurement points in time, and accumulated investments made to reduce these quantities

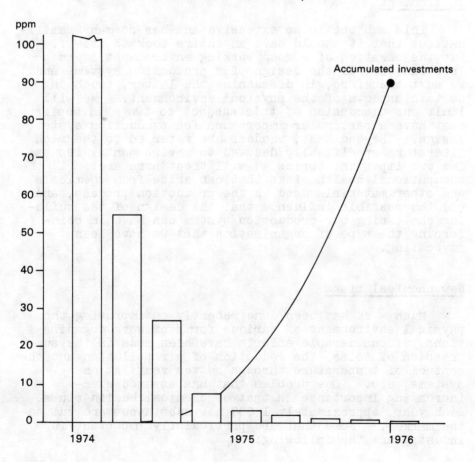

In the design of a production system, it is imperative for all substances contained in raw materials or used in work processes to be carefully screened to see whether any of them may present a health hazard. If such hazards are found, then certain measures have to be taken, such as:

- <u>Changing the production conditions</u>. For example, the content of dangerous substances in the products manufactured can be minimised. This may sometimes have a negative effect on the function of the end products and in some cases also on manufacturing costs.

- <u>Choosing suitable equipment</u>. Production equipment can be designed so that shielding, exhaust intakes or other devices to reduce risks may be installed.

- <u>Encapsulation</u>. In particularly dangerous situations the process can be designed so as to take place entirely enclosed in a special housing equipped with the necessary input and output points, etc.

- <u>Preventing pollution</u>. Some possible ways of preventing pollution are choosing a different process technology, using different raw materials, and altering the composition of the materials used.

- <u>Preventing the spreading of chemical pollution</u>. This can be achieved through mechanisation or automation. Figure 18 shows some examples of how the undesirable spreading of light substances can be prevented by using air curtains.

These questions cannot under any circumstances be avoided in designing a production system. It is considerably easier to find good solutions to the problems while a new system is being planned than when they are allowed to arise after a system has been put into operation.

The small factory

A recurrent theme in our discussion has been the desirability of giving small systems a high degree of self-sufficiency. Even in the design of the building that shelters the production system, there is much to be said for giving this "small factory" idea a high priority.

If we compare a factory in which 1,000 persons work under conventional organisational conditions with another factory in which 1,000 persons are grouped in 10 smaller production systems, each constituting an independent

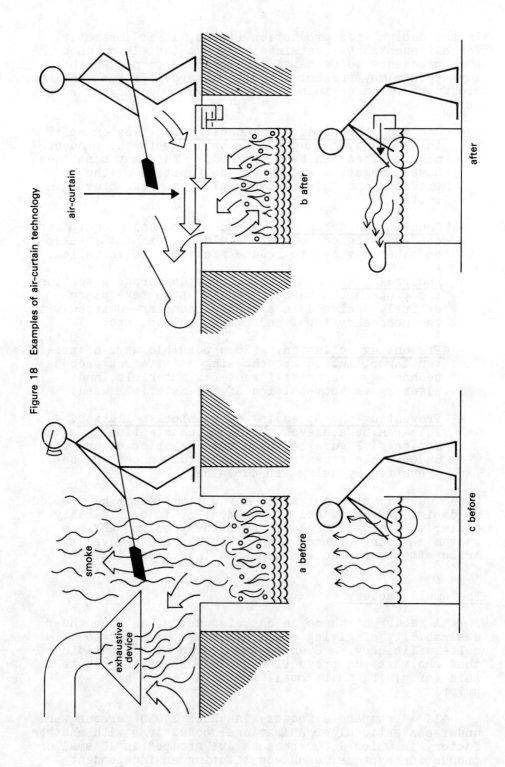

Figure 18 Examples of air-curtain technology

air-curtain

smoke

exhaustive device

b after

a before

after

c before

product factory, we shall see numerous advantages in the second alternative. In the small factory, it is easier to create attractive working conditions and job involvement for those working there. The small building helps create a "we" feeling that facilitates contacts between co-workers. Moreover, lighting and noise problems are easier to solve, and it is simpler to give the building a more aesthetic character and better adaptability to the natural surroundings.

There are two principal ways of creating "the small factory":

- small, free-standing buildings;

- "small-scale" design and the physical proximity of members of groups in larger buildings.

If it is possible to divide up production in a natural way to take place in several small buildings, this is obviously the solution that most clearly stresses independence of units and that gives employees the best overall view of an entire production unit.

Let us look at one example of such a way of dividing up a factory. At the factory of Svenska Fläktfabriken in Ljungarum, Sweden, the building was constructed with a number of modules or "standard blocks" in order to generate a small-scale feeling, harmonising better with human needs than a more orthodox large-scale construction (figure 19). The design is similar to that of a squarish city plan with streets and blocks marked out. This very clear and simple pattern makes it easy to feel at home and orient oneself, even if the work area in question is relatively large. Each standard block consists of two two-aisled workshops, connected to service buildings (offices, changing room, coffee rooms, cafeterias, etc.). The total area is about 10,000 square metres. Approximately 200 persons work in each standard block. Since even the administration facilities have been placed in the factory, and the organisation is based on products, each production plant or standard block can function in comparative independence of its environment.

The outstanding example of how small shops can be designed into one large building is Volvo's Kalmar factory, which we mentioned earlier in another connection. Its design is shown in figure 20. This ingenious design has made it possible to give each production group its own area with its own entrance and personnel facilities, even though the production groups are a part of a larger flow that runs through the entire factory. Parts inventories in the middle of the building supply production groups with materials. The areas of the various groups

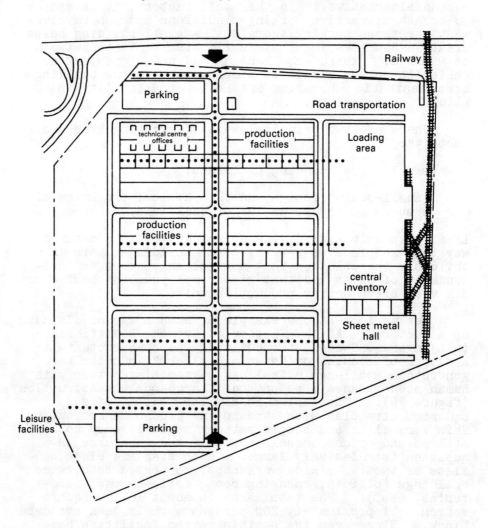

Figure 19   Factory plan with standard blocks

.are strung out along the outer walls of the building.
In most cases there are windows giving a view of the
natural surroundings.   There are about 30 work groups,
with about 15 to 20 persons in each.

This effort to stress the "small factory" in the
design of the building itself can provide a suitable concluding note to our discussion.   Small factories,
simple, safe and efficient factories, pleasant and
attractive factories - these are the lines of thinking
we have wanted to emphasise in our discussion of the
design of production systems, for new and better forms of
work organisation.

Figure 20   Over-all view of Volvo's Kalmar factory

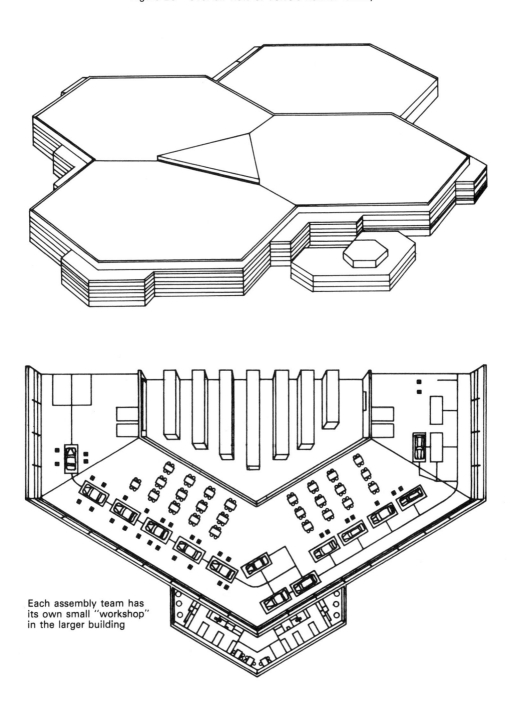

Each assembly team has
its own small "workshop"
in the larger building

THE IMPACT OF JOB REFORM ON ACCOUNTING SYSTEMS

3

Anders Malmberg*

1.   Introduction

During the past few years, many companies have been developing, and experimenting with, new production systems deriving from the new approaches and new lines of thinking that have been discussed earlier in this book. With the help of four criteria - good production systems, independence in small systems, stable and fluctuation-resistant operation, and attractive jobs in a good working environment - efforts have been made both to increase productivity and to improve the work situation.

When these ideas are put into actual practice, the problem arises of suitable changes and corresponding modifications in various administrative procedures.   If progress on the administrative side does not keep pace with progress in production systems, the advantage of new working methods cannot be fully realised.   We will discuss here some of the ways in which budgeting and accounting systems will be influenced by these new forms of work organisation.

Our discussion thus takes from developments in working situation as its starting point.   We are not attempting to present a complete analysis of problems and solutions in financial reporting.   We shall limit our discussion to some of the issues that are particularly important in the development of new job design and new forms of work organisation.

---

*   Swedish Management Group.

2. Why fresh thinking is needed in accounting

Far-reaching innovations have been taking place during recent years in company administrative and organisational structures. The traditional functionally oriented organisation has been gradually giving way to the product- and results-oriented organisational model. A main objective has been to concentrate responsibility for the results of different types of activity and product areas at points in the organisation where they are most logical and meaningful. This decentralisation process has altered the over-all organisational structure of virtually all medium-sized and large companies.

Innovations in forms of work organisation have not only been moving from the top down. Equally important signs of evolution have been taking place further down.

Team work, production groups and product shops are some of the central concepts in this process. An increasingly common goal has been the development of production operations in independent smaller units. Not least important, these organisational changes have been discussed in terms of their significance for intensified participation by workers and increased autonomy for work groups.

Changes in the work organisation and company administrative procedures, however, have up to now had scarcely any influence on accounting practices. To be sure, some new demands and needs have been satisfied. This has been particularly true at the upper levels, where efforts have been made to adapt the accounting and reporting systems to the new form of organisation. But in many respects old practices have lived on, despite their incompatibility with the evolution of organisational and managerial thinking.

When new production groups have been introduced, considerable difficulty has often been experienced in meeting the new demands in a comprehensive, integrated accounting system. To avoid upsetting the over-all system in the company, individual units have had to muddle through with the use of ad hoc manual routines and have often had to get along without some parts of the information that had been judged essential.

The slower pace that has characterised the adaptation of financial systems to the new demands of smaller semi-autonomous groups is not too encouraging. There is an urgent need to bring about a rapid renewal of attitudes, systems and routines that can support the development of new working methods and production practices.   And this renewal must be carried out in close collaboration with the <u>users</u> of information who are affected.

3.   Recent developments in budgeting and accounting

Budgeting and accounting have been undergoing some profound changes.   Internal reporting has become more detailed and more closely adapted to realistic company models.   Computerisation has created new opportunities for the collection and processing of information for various reports and calculations.   Budgeting has progressed considerably as a result of these advances, and also as a result of needs to solve current problems in companies.   The trend has been towards a systematisation and formalisation of the budgeting function. Increasingly advanced models of computation and budgeting have had to be developed so that the figures shall accurately reflect company activities.

The driving force behind this development has usually come from specialists in the company's financial and data processing departments.   The problems and needs that have been given the closest attention are those that the specialists themselves have experienced.   Problems and efforts to find solutions have only rarely been discussed with those in the company who are actually the users of the information.   Moreover, many users have lacked knowledge and understanding of over-all needs in reporting.   New routines and systems have therefore often been met with scepticism or with a "we don't need that kind of thing" reaction.

Modern accounting systems have been developed essentially to fulfil the following primary tasks:

- calculation of the company's profit or loss;

- price-setting computations and profitability analyses of individual products;

- control of productivity through comparisons of calculated and actual production costs.

These tasks continue to be important, but new needs for financial information and analysis have arisen.   The newer types of management and work organisation call for the active participation of numerous persons in planning and decision-making functions.   Responsibility and authority have been delegated and new problems and new conditions have arisen.

The remainder of this chapter will be devoted to a
discussion of some of the new demands on a company's
financial systems and their consequences. We will
discuss some of the various lines of development and
illustrate them with examples from two Swedish companies.

4. Accounting for small
    independent production units

During the last decade, many organisations and jobs
have developed in such a way as to increase the participation of work groups and their individual members in the
design of their work. This trend is expected to
continue. In the area of production planning and
control, this means that the employees in departments,
workshops, etc., will participate more and more in both
the planning and the control procedures. Primarily they
ought to be engaged in the budgetary work concerning
their own unit as well, since budgeting is closely
related to this process. Both the employees and the
company can benefit from this participation.

In the future it will be important to have access,
with a view to supplementing present reporting practices,
to concepts and routines that can adequately describe
financial problems and results within small units. It
is vital for managers and employees to be able to understand the connection between, on the one hand, their own
situation and their own jobs, and, on the other, the
financial development of the company.

So as to emphasise and facilitate participation of
the workers and increased autonomy for small units,
various types of measures can be taken within the
accounting function. Examples of these are improved
basic financial information for work planning and the
education of employees in financial matters. If we are
to design new production systems, we must have reporting
routines that focus on the working group and its tasks.
It must be possible to produce financial results that are
directly related to the various manufacturing operations.
To achieve this goal, we must set up new accounting
systems that are capable of:

- measuring and computing the working group's
  financial results;

- meeting the need for financial information that is
  required for work and for production planning;

- granting the working groups increased influence on
  their own reporting activities.

Many aspects of today's accounting systems will retain their importance in the future, since they satisfy the need for information at the highest level of the company. In the area of financial planning, for instance, top management has to analyse cash flow and make proper financial arrangements. Top management has also to make decisions concerning capital markets, borrowing and capitalisation. These issues do not usually affect the different working units directly. The need for, or the benefit from the participation of the workers in this part of reporting and planning is not so obvious. What is more obvious is the need for developing new methods dealing with the financial reporting requirements of lower-level management.

The practicability and difficulty of measuring financial results in small units varies widely from one company to another, depending on the type of organisation and the nature of the production operation. In the past, there has been scarcely any development or use of internal financial measurements, except in large units, such as divisions within a company. In such cases, the focus continues to be on an over-all evaluation with the calculation of profit and loss or profitability. If any financial reports for departments and working groups exist, these have to be in a simpler form. Usually, reference is made to responsibility for costs, and the figures used are budgeted costs. As a complement to such practices, many managers have created their own informal reporting practices, often in the form of "little black books".

If we are to create considerably greater independence for smaller units such as supervisory areas and product shops, or working groups, we must develop better reporting practices. We need new methods with simple, comprehensive measures of results that take into consideration the utilisation of resources, productivity, and the value of production. We must develop practical models showing how a supervisor, for example, can construct a system of accounting and reporting that will make it possible for him and his co-workers to keep a continuous check on their financial situation and decide themselves on what should be done in order to reach the financial goals.

In connection with the introduction of new forms of work organisation a number of Swedish companies have encountered the need for better financial reporting in small production units. We will look at two approaches to the improved measurement of results in such units, taken from the actual experience of Swedish companies.

5. Internal financial reporting in a rubber factory

In the company in question, a new system of
production reporting was introduced, partly because of
difficulties experienced over a period of years in
adhering to projected calculations, and partly with a
view to tracing the sources of deviations from these
calculations. Production was therefore broken down into
a number of "self-sufficient" units where revenues and
costs could be accurately allotted to each. One result
of the new system was that the negative deviations from
the pre-set targets were dramatically reduced. One
reason for its success was that many more workers became
conscious of, and involved in, the ways in which their
own work influenced the financial results.

The company produces moulded rubber components.
Two-thirds of production, gaskets for pipes and axles, is
used for the company's own products, and one-third is
intended for subcontracting. In 1977, there were 500
employees, and sales reached more than 90 million Swedish
crowns. Production is divided into nine units, that is,
production groups, each with its own reporting function.
Three of the units produce semi-fabricated products and
six finished products.

Every order undergoes a meticulous production-
planning process. This is the point where internal
reporting comes into the picture. The system makes it
possible for every production group that works on an
order to make sure that it is producing a profit.

Preliminary calculations, the basis for internal reporting

Let us take a concrete example. It begins with a
query from a customer on the cost of a certain type of
seal. The production-planning section checks to see
that the specified measurements and tolerances are
reasonable. With advanced machine-tool design, the
item can be produced semi-automatically, which results
in a very low cost per unit. Such a machine tool,
however, would be too costly for production involving
small runs. The company therefore proposes another
manufacturing method, which calls for more stages of
work, but lower investment in equipment.

Once the problem of equipment is solved, production
is planned and the price of the product is computed in a
preliminary way. Acceptance by the customer of the
quotation means that an agreement is reached. Payment
is thus made on the basis of the pre-calculation and not

the actual cost.   This is the customary relation between buyer and seller.   The buyer wants to know in advance what the item will cost, and the seller must be able to produce the item at the price he promised the buyer in order to avoid losing money.   In the present rubber factory, this is true for the company as a whole, and also for production groups, since they are organised and financially autonomous units.

Production groups are profit centres with calculations of profit and loss on every order

The previous accounting system was also based on calculated costs for each order and product.   Pre-calculations were compared with actual costs for the factory as a whole.   Only certain costs were allocated by departments and other units.   It was not possible, therefore, to see where in the organisation the deviation had occurred.   In the new accounting system the production groups are allotted their portion of the pre-calculated price.   If they do the job more efficiently than calculated, the cost is lower and the group registers a profit.   The deviation from the calculation is positive.   In this way, each production group becomes a profit centre that can operate at a profit or a loss in relation to the figure included in the pre-calculated price.

To return to the example of the seal.   According to the calculated quotation, it is possible to determine in advance what each group working on the order shall be "paid" for its work and for the materials it will use.

Three working groups participate in the production of the seal:

- the mixing group, which prepares the material to be used in the seal - i.e., the mixture of rubber;

- the product material group, which, for each unit, sprays the rubber mixture in the proper thickness and length;

- the moulding group, which presses and vulcanises the material into the finished form of the seal.

Production groups "sell" their production to each other at pre-calculated standard prices

Transfer between groups is effected in such a way that each group "sells" its "product" to the next group in the processing chain. It begins with a requisition from the mixing group for the materials needed from the raw materials inventory; it does the mixing and then "sells" it to the product materials group at the pre-calculated price per kilogram. The pre-calculation, which determines how much the mixing group will be paid per kilogram on delivery to the product material group, covers materials, plus a certain allowance for waste, and a wage-based cost for the time normally called for in the mixing operation.

At the end, the finished seals are produced by the moulding group. The pre-calculation includes a standard price for the direct work and a standard price for the finished product. To whom does the moulding group sell? Not to the customer, but to the marketing department. In making the original quotation, the marketing department has included the pre-calculated total manufacturing cost - the standard manufacturing cost, or SMC - and added an amount for sales and overheads.

The SMC serves as a calculated price between production and the marketing department, and is already fixed in the pre-calculation stage. This is important, because the effects of productivity then remain in the production process and show up as deviations from the pre-calculation. In this way, the production departments can see the results of their efforts to work efficiently, and the profit or loss will show up in the internal reporting of production costs.

The order for the seal is therefore the origin of a chain of internal transactions between the units. The sequence is illustrated in figure 1.

Workers can influence their results through their own efforts

If the personnel in the mixing group can reduce waste by being more careful, they can produce more of the mixture from a given quantity of raw materials in relation to pre-calculations. Or, to put it in another way, a profit can be made by producing a mixture at a lower price per kilogram than projected. From a technical reporting point of view, the actual materials consumption for the seals, compared with the pre-calculated direct materials use, can be shown as follows:

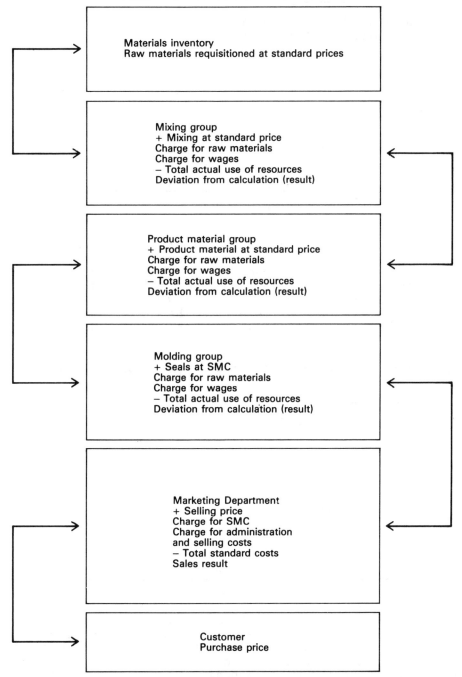

Figure 1   Chain of transactions between units

Materials inventory
Raw materials requisitioned at standard prices

Mixing group
+ Mixing at standard price
Charge for raw materials
Charge for wages
− Total actual use of resources
Deviation from calculation (result)

Product material group
+ Product material at standard price
Charge for raw materials
Charge for wages
− Total actual use of resources
Deviation from calculation (result)

Molding group
+ Seals at SMC
Charge for raw materials
Charge for wages
− Total actual use of resources
Deviation from calculation (result)

Marketing Department
+ Selling price
Charge for SMC
Charge for administration
and selling costs
− Total standard costs
Sales result

Customer
Purchase price

<u>Income (credit)</u>

Quantity delivered multiplied by
pre-calculated standard price per
kilo for direct materials

500 kg x 4,50 crowns		= 2 250 cr.

<u>Costs (debit)</u>

Quantity of raw materials taken
from inventory at standard price
per kilo

525 kg x 4,50 crowns	= 2 362 cr.

Deviation from calculation, direct materials	112 cr.

To proceed with our calculation: if the materials
cost for the mixture and the time costs together are less
than the standard price received when the materials are
sold, the product material group shows a profit. As
indicated above, it is the use of raw materials ("as much
product material as possible from the mixture materials")
plus time that determines whether the result will be
positive or negative.

Deviations from projected times are reported as follows:

<u>Income (credit)</u>

Quantity delivered multiplied by
pre-calculated standard wage for
direct work

500 kg x 1 crown	500 cr.

<u>Costs (debit)</u>

Direct time worked multiplied by
standard wage cost

19 hrs x 25 crowns	475 cr.

Deviation from calculation for direct work	25 cr.

As can be seen the profits of the production groups
can be derived either through the efficient use of raw
materials or through efficient work. Within the groups,
there is naturally a desire to "make ends meet" - that
is, to complete the work according to the pre-calculation.
If they succeed, they have done their part so that the
company can continue to exist and operate according to
prevailing market conditions.

Internal financial statements
eight times per year

In this company, the deviation in the financial
results of the nine manufacturing groups is computed and
reported eight times a year. This internal financial
reporting is done for periods of six working weeks at a
time. On the last day of each period, a record of goods
in process, quantities of materials used and working time
registered is drawn up. Through the participation of
everyone in this keeping of inventory records according
to a fixed schedule, the whole procedure can be finished
in a few hours.

The period report can be compiled as shown in
figure 2 on the basis of these records of materials
received and delivered at standard prices and of direct
wage costs and variable other costs:

Figure 2   Report on production results

PRODUCTION RESULT per 6-week period							
Production group: Moulding						Period 7	
This period					Analysis of deviations from calculations	From beginning	
Rubber	Other dir. mat'ls	Sub-contract	Dir. wages	Suppl. costs		Rubber	Other mat'ls
810	325	4	295	340	Standard manufacturing cost (SMC)	5170	2
750	300	5	300	350	Charges: Period's costs	5000	
200	70	–	50	60	+ starting relation materials/in-process goods	250	
150	40	–	60	65	– finishing relation materials/in-process goods		
800	330	5	290	345	Total actual mfg cost		
+ 10	– 5	– 1	+ 5	– 5	Deviation from calculation		

The actual manufacturing costs in a group are
derived from direct materials - rubber, other direct
materials, subcontracted materials - direct wages and
supplementary charges. Supplementary charges include
auxiliary wage costs, indirect materials used, energy
and maintenance, and also fixed charges such as
depreciation and calculated interest costs. These costs
are compared with those that should have been registered
according to pre-calculations, that is, the standard
manufacturing cost (SMC).

At this point, it is possible to make interesting
analyses of the deviations of actual costs from standard
costs. In many cases, it appears that, for example, a

positive deviation in wages is offset by a negative
deviation in materials used. Conversely, high positive
materials deviations may be matched by negative wages
deviations. We therefore find that sometimes careful
work, which saves on materials, results in more time
worked, which is quite natural.

Internal reports are studied by the entire production group

About three weeks after the end of each period, the
financial and production departments and all production
supervisors are called together to analyse the production
results. The outcome is discussed and commented upon
and everyday problems are taken up, along with whatever
corrective measures are indicated by the figures. The
purpose of the meetings is primarily to make the workers
conscious, each in his own way, of the common result.

Within the groups, each production supervisor
informs his co-workers of the discussions. The
experience with this system is very good. One supervisor says that this accounting system has changed his
job. After meeting with his workers, he finds that
they all understand the system. Orders for raw
materials, time reports and other operation documents
are correctly handled. The workers know that these
figures are financial realities. Each worker takes
charge of his own job and the supervisor assists where he
is needed. Greater responsibility and his participation
in decisions and plans for his working group, provide a
worker with some positive motivation and increase his
satisfaction at work.

6. Internal financial reporting for a wholesale distributor

A new reporting system was set up in the financial
department of a certain wholesaler. Discussions were
held with various operating units to ascertain the
financial information they needed. Eventually, this led
to the type of analysis that we will describe here.
This example shows how continuing internal reporting can
be adapted to the information needs of working groups and
other individual units.

Why develop new financial routines?

At the point where our examination of this case
begins, systematic planning and reporting had been
practised for five years. This began with simple

routines for budgeting, and gradually other systems for
keeping track of financial developments were added. As
the system evolved, the recognition of new problems grew,
and opportunities were seen for making some parts of the
operation, such as sales and inventory control, more
efficient. Certain parts of the planning and reporting
routines had been developed more than others. For
example, great pains had been taken with income
budgeting, but cost and investment budgeting lagged
somewhat behind.

One of the fundamental problems seemed to be that
too little was known about the <u>relations</u> between the
flow of goods through the warehouses, the operations
involved in this flow and the need for and use of
resources connected with these operations. The
situation can be illustrated by figure 3.

Figure 3   Flow of goods, operations and need for resources

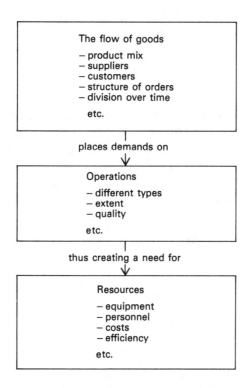

How could a better view be obtained of the activities in
different departments and the relations between the flow
of goods and the use of resources? How could the
information supplied through financial reporting be used
most advantageously?

The reporting system functioning at that time was not adapted to this type of operations planning. It was primarily intended for measuring the results of the sales department. Indeed, this reporting system produced virtually complete profit calculations for various groups of goods. For a trading company, this was extremely useful information. But a negative factor was that the reporting produced practically no information for use in planning and following up current operations. It was difficult to analyse the utilisation of capacity and of resources when accounting figures indicated only how costs ought to be distributed among different products.

The question then arose of the changes that could be made in the accounting system so that it could be useful in operations planning. It appeared to be difficult to change the reporting system without affecting the product calculations. Instead, it was decided to expand the internal reporting activity in two directions; towards a product-oriented information system and towards an operations-oriented system. The latter could be adapted to the special needs of operations planning and follow-up activities.

Organising operations in a warehouse

In order to develop the operations-oriented reporting system, it was necessary to conduct a careful study showing the factors that were of significance in producing a true picture of the relations between the product flow, the operations involved in this flow and the resources. Surveys were thus made of sales, inventory control, transport and administration.

We will now describe the results of this analysis, and show how the system turned out, using the example of the new methods developed for inventory control. In addition to inventory control the operation department in the company is responsible for the delivery of goods to customers, internal transport, some preparation of goods and the loading and unloading of incoming and outgoing goods. Under the old reporting system, there had been no clear division between these activities in the operating department. Now, it was deemed important to draw up special reports on the costs of each of them. In a wholesaler's warehouse, there is a torrential flood of various goods and products that are continuously streaming through. Deliveries to the warehouse consist of large quantities of the same product, while shipments out are most often relatively small quantities of many different products. The volume of goods in inventory varies with the seasons and with economic cycles.

The warehouse in question, which employs about 100 persons, is divided into different sections. In each section, goods with similar handling characteristics (shape, weight, fragility, etc.) are stored together and the goods can be classified into different types of products. Equipment for handling and storing goods is adapted to their particular characteristics. Some members of the workforce are permanently stationed in different sections, while others move from section to section according to needs. Time worked in each section serves as the basis for calculating the piece-work wage payments.

The determining factor in the use of time is primarily the volume of goods that must be received and shipped. The reception work depends on the quantities received, and the shipping time varies with the number of separate shipments. That is, it makes no difference whether a shipment weighs 500 kilograms or 2 tons. In both cases, it is handled as one package. Time used in reception may therefore be said to be roughly proportionate to the number of tons and time used in shipping proportionate to the number of shipments.

Information for financial reporting

After looking at the over-all operation in this way, it was possible to discuss the type of information needed for planning and follow-up. The demands whose satisfaction was considered necessary in the new internal reporting system are given below:

- It must be possible to relate the information to the different types of operations or functions that are carried out in a department.

- Figures on resources and costs do not suffice. For meaningful assessments to be made, the use of resources must be matched to the achievements and results registered during a certain period.

- The use of resources needs to be measured not only in money terms. In order to assess the efficiency of a unit, it is often better to consider the efforts of the workforce in terms of time worked.

Inventory control forms a group of activities within the operating department. If the use of resources and the quantity of work done are to be assessed, it is desirable for the reporting to include figures on both costs (time worked) and goods handled in the warehouse.

It was proposed that the following should be measured and recorded for internal reporting purposes:

Flow of goods

- number of tons received per section;
- number of shipments made per section;
- average inventory in tons per section.

Use of resources

- number of hours worked per section;
- total wage costs for warehouse;
- tool costs per section;
- packaging costs per section;
- materials costs consumed per section;
- repairs and maintenance costs per section.

Productivity

- number of tons received per hour for each section;
- number of shipments loaded per hour for each section.

The proposal entailed a number of improvements over the old reporting system. The following changes were seen to be especially important:

- costs were to be related to operations within the department;
- the efforts of employees were to be measured both as time and as wage costs;
- measurements of work results would be more meaningful than those obtained from sales and purchasing statistics;
- the measurement unit "shipments loaded" would be more relevant than tons sold;
- the flow of goods was to be measured per section instead of per product group, as previously. When products in the same product group are stored in different sections, the old statistics are inaccurate;

- information on the flow of goods was to be based on reception and shipment documents. Earlier, it was necessary to refer to invoices for this information, and in terms of time these do not ordinarily correspond to deliveries;

- through a proper division of costs, each section was to be charged only for the costs that it could influence. In the case of common resources, or when decisions are made at a higher level, costs are related to the operating department or the unit where the decision is made.

The reporting of these figures on the operations of the company made it possible to develop new follow-up reports, in which interesting and financially meaningful information on operations could be presented in a simple and easily understandable table. This made it possible for managers and workers in the different sections to become involved in planning and controlling activities in a completely new way. Let us look at a sample monthly report from the inventory management function (figure 4). Similar reports are prepared for shipments to customers, internal transport and other activities within the department.

In such a report, department management can follow developments month by month in the different sections. Information is reported on hours worked, on the use of materials and other costs and on the quantities of goods that have been handled. In order to measure productivity, average volume per hour worked can be used. Full information for the most recent period and the cumulative total from the beginning of the year are both given. Actual figures and deviations from budget are included.

Since these reports contain information adapted to management responsibilities at a low organisational level, they are understandable and useful for supervisors and workers. This makes it possible for the personnel in the warehouse to participate in the budgetary control work.

7. Internal financial reporting:
   A necessity for independent
   production units

If a production unit or department is to be independent and to have a "life" of its own with which workers can identify themselves and for which they can feel responsible, the activities of the unit must be reported separately from those of all other departments. The reporting must make it possible for each worker

Figure 4 Sample inventory management report

OPERATIONS REPORT, MARCH

OPERATING DEPARTMENT	MARCH				FROM BEGINNING OF YEAR		
	Use of resources		Results		Use of resources		Results
INVENTORY MANAGEMENT							
Costs in thousand crowns	Actual	Deviation from budget %	Actual	Deviation from budget %	Actual	Deviation from budget %	Actual
Section long goods							
hours worked	386	+ 8			1110	+ 4	
costs for packaging	2.6	+ 3			7.0	± 0	
tools	1.0	+ 10			2.5	+ 4	
materials used	1.2	– 7			4.3	– 3	
repairs and maintenance	2.7	+ 150			5.1	+ 42	
total costs incl. wages	19.1	+ 12			54.7	+ 8	
tons received			764	– 7			
shipments loaded			465	+ 4			
productivity							
reception tons/hr			0.25	+ 20			
shipments/hr			0.42	+ 5			
Section rolled goods							
.							
.							
.							
.							
Inventory management total							
hours worked	6180	+ 3			19.1		
wage costs including social charges	191.6	+ 7			59		
costs for packaging	33.0	+ 3			8		
tools	10.6	– 8					
materials used	14.2	+ 4					
repairs and maintenance	9.2	+ 40					
total costs	258.6	+ 5					
tons received			16180	+ 2			
shipments loaded			9640	+ 5			

to see his own department as an autonomous unit - with its own physical space, technical equipment, personnel, scheduled capacity, and so on. It must be possible to see what its costs are and how these costs are further included in other calculations and are compensated for by the prices asked for the company's products.

Most medium-sized and big companies do not have accounting systems designed to give information at such a detailed level. As budgeting and accounting have been mostly used by management at higher organisational levels, the accounting information is usually more aggregated. Therefore the development of internal financial reporting for small units is a very important issue.

The examples from the rubber company and the whole-sale company have shown two ways of adapting reporting to the need for follow-up information within different production units. The examples differ in some important respects. In the rubber factory, the reporting pro-cedure is built round the products and sales orders corresponding to manufacturing activities. The result measured in financial terms includes actual costs related to pre-calculated costs. The use of the profit-centre concept at this low level of management illustrates a simple way of giving the supervisor and his production group understandable and useful information.

In respect of the wholesale company it was shown that a product and profitability oriented system cannot always fulfil the need for follow-up information within operating units. In this company middle and lower management had access to information on the financial consequences of different operations. The new account-ing system is based on the different activities performed in the warehouse. Information that contains more than merely financial data - for example data on physical volumes of goods - is reported separately for each type of activity. The result is measured in several comple-mentary ways in the form of key figures.

The two cases illustrate the need for more detailed information in production units. But the collected and reported data differ because of the different types of operation. The type of information and the way of measuring results must be adapted to the operation in question.

The determining factor in deciding what information should be set forth in internal reporting is the way in which those within a production group can influence the outcome of production. For example, if manufacturing is rigidly machine-paced, then attention should be directed

to the capacity utilisation of the machine.   In manufacturing complex and costly products, breakage and capital
tied up in in-process goods are central elements.   In
assembly work and other work in which manual activity is
important, hours worked and productivity are especially
significant.   In the design of internal financial
recording and reporting procedures in a particular
company, the factors that are financially meaningful and
subject to influence in different production units must
be selected for use.   The information thus produced can
form the basis for the design of the reporting system.

8.   <u>Some final key questions</u>

     A workable method of measuring and computing
financial results for a small production unit is probably
the most important reporting issue in granting increased
independence to small units.   But other financial
questions are also important in this connection.   As a
conclusion to our discussion of the adaptation of
reporting systems to new types of production design, we
will very briefly look at two of these issues.   They
have begun to receive attention only recently, with the
development of interest in issues concerning working life
in general.   Although we can discern some general
principles that might lead to practicable solutions,
there is as yet scarcely any solid experience to show how
these problems can be realistically attached in companies.

<u>Independence of the reporting
system within a smaller
organisational unit</u>

     The possibilities of dividing up large factories or
continuous production lines into small "autonomous
companies" or "autonomous groups", can be realised from
the production point of view in many cases.   It is
important as well, to increase the independence of these
units, factories, product shops, supervisor areas, flow
groups and the like, by giving them additional responsibility.

     One of the factors that determine the independence
of a unit is its degree of self-sufficiency, that is, the
degree to which the unit has its own resources for
performing different tasks and solving different problems.
There are various ways of increasing this degree of self-
sufficiency.   In small production units it can be
increased by equipping them with their own production of
service resources.   This point has been discussed in the
previous chapter.   However, the possession of independent administrative resources for such activities as

financial record-keeping, materials delivery and personnel administration also contributes to an increased
degree of self-sufficiency for the small unit.

The reporting of costs for a small unit, or a
production department in a company, is an integral part
of a larger reporting system for the whole company.
This reporting system is in turn inter-connected with a
number of other financial administrative systems, such as
billing, computing wages, etc.

When work is started on the development of new forms
of organisation within a department and it is recognised
that a new system for financial reporting is needed, one
large practical difficulty is encountered immediately:
A partial system for a small unit cannot be reorganised
because it will disturb the entire over-all system.
Certain primary information must still be collected in
the future, certain processing routines must be carried
through, and so on.   When these questions are studied,
a provocative conclusion is likely to present itself:
The reporting system for a company is so completely
integrated and so complex that it is impossible to change
only one small part of it!

Naturally, this situation is unacceptable.   If we
want to change a number of financial systems, we must
learn to change them bit by bit.   The only alternative
is to change everything at once, and in that case no
genuinely new forms could ever be developed in a reasonable amount of time.   We must therefore learn to
"set free" the reporting system in a small unit, to
revitalise that unit without disturbing the over-all
system, to construct the new system one piece at a time.
One objective in this work must be to give the smaller
units increased independence and responsibility for their
own administrative routines.

Active participation in budgeting, and inter-relation between different organisational levels in this process

In the preparation of a budget, the main lines of
the following year's activities must be drawn up.   If
planning decisions are to contribute to efficient
operations in the whole company, the budgeting work must
include smooth co-ordination between all units in the
company.

In the development of new forms of work organisation,
there remains of course a need for reasonable co-
ordination between the different working groups or units.
But completely new demands must also be met.   Many more

persons must be involved in financial planning and
budgeting, since it is at the working group level that
several decisions can be made particularly regarding
short-term goals.   Furthermore, individual units in the
company are encouraged far more than in the past to plot
their own development - albeit within a given framework.

Finding an optimum equilibrium in the budgeting
process between the independence of local units and
demands for a reasonable degree of co-ordination and at
the same time involving considerably more workers in the
process is an important issue in the development of new
systems for financial reporting.   One of the problems is
to bring about a dialogue, a continuing interaction
between different organisational levels during the
construction of the budget.   A process must be created
in which both local perspectives and over-all co-
ordination imperatives can be combined to reach effective
and broadly workable financial goals.

PERSONNEL IMPLICATIONS FOR MANAGEMENT OF NEW FORMS OF WORK ORGANISATION

4

Nitish De*

The employment question is going to be one of the major problems of our time. Quantitatively, we want the number of job opportunities in a country more or less consistent with the number of people who want to work. Achieving this goal of full employment will require qualitative changes in how we organise work, the conditions under which it is performed and the attitudes we develop in ourselves and our children about it.

So far we have made little effort to create meaningful jobs in white-collar occupations. Just as humans have come to serve the machine in production so too have attempts to make administration more effective failed: so far, most of the things done in offices in the name of "efficiency" simply narrow the work content and debase the human contribution ....

Gyllenhammar[1]

1. The personnel function: Its traditional roles

The personnel function is conceived as a staff activity distinct from line activities, although, in a complex organisation, so clear-cut a distinction cannot be sustained. In recent years, there has been a spurt of staff work and intake of staff personnel in many organisations.[2] The personnel function organised under a distinct staff group has been one of the oldest in origin. Whereas the chronology of its functional roles

---

* Director, Public Enterprises Centre for Continuing Education, New Delhi, India.

has not followed a uniform pattern, by and large, it has
derived its legitimacy from the following needs:

(a) to respond to government rules, regulations and in-
junctions;

(b) to develop strategies and tactics to deal with trade
union demands and pressures and industrial action;

(c) to "service" the employing departments with a view
to keeping employees in a suitable state of work
discipline through various measures, such as, appropriate selection, induction and training systems,
the maintenance of personnel records, benefit
schemes or monitoring systems.

In essence, the personnel function has been primarily concerned, directly or indirectly, with the
"interest-related" issues, while the "work-related"
issues have become the concern of direct management (the
line function). The implications of this broad division
of labour are the following:

(a) the personnel function has remained divorced from a
dynamic appreciation of some of the key organisational tasks: technology and its utilisation;
products and markets; finance; planning machinery
and so on;

(b) its "appreciative system" of the changing environment has remained confined to limited segments, such
as, the trade union movement, labour economics data
or the labour market;

(c) its role has ranged essentially from maintenance
orientation to reactive orientation. There has
been dependence on past experience and established
conventions;

(d) there has been a disposition towards job specialisation and sub-grouping of tasks - union negotiations,
establishment matters, training, recruitment, industrial relations machinery, legal aspects of industrial disputes, grievance handling, personnel audit
functions, etc.;

(e) in a power-oriented hierarchical system, the
advisory function is subjected at times to manipulative pressure through the use of trade unions as a
handle to "control" management. In the process,
there is an identity crisis about the clientele -
management or trade union or employees or all.
This may take the form of shifting loyalty, depending on the exigency of the situation;

(f) by and large, research as a personnel function
    remains a low priority job. Knowledge of human
    science and systems literature receives inadequate
    attention.

These implications do not apply necessarily to all
organisations, but implicitly or otherwise some of them
do characterise the operation of the personnel function.

2.   A new approach to the personnel function

Let us, on the basis of what has been stated so far,
assume that the traditional roles of the personnel function must be recast because of the need to regard employees in an organisation as active and learning entities.
The shift that is necessary in the personnel function
will take place at several levels. To begin with,
there will be a need for the personnel men to orient
themselves towards a new gestalt of the purposes of human
organisations. A human system, in a rapidly changing
environment, is to be conceived as tending towards ideal-
seeking where it can offer an open-system "problemising"
type of learning. Human efforts, in such a situation,
are to be directed towards being "with the world" rather
than merely "in the world", so that a critical conscious-
ness of reality can be created in the organisation. The
nature of man is to be conceived in terms of such ideals
as nurturance (cultivation and growth of people - self
and others), homonomy (a sense of relatedness and belong-
ingness to oneself and others), humanity (man as the end
measure) and beauty (aesthetic state). In terms of
organisation values, such an orientation will imply that
there has to be a transition from achievement to self-
actualisation, from independence to interdependence, from
self-control to self-expression and from endurance of
denial to capacity for joy.[3] Faith and hope in these
values are suggested as the first requisite for personnel
functionaries.

Secondly, such ideals should be conceived in the
context of an ecological balance of physical environment
and human environment. The notion that organisational
viability requires the exploitation of the physical
environment to fulfil human needs has to be replaced by
a sense of dynamic equilibrium between the gifts of
nature and the conversion of these gifts into the use
value of goods and services. Within this context issues
such as the concern of the environmentalists for
preservation of natural resources are to be viewed as an
essential requirement for the survival and preservation
of mankind.

Thirdly, as a sequel to the earlier two propositions, there will be a need to view an organisation in terms of a complex dynamic equilibrium of many organisation systems.   This may be thought of as being aware of "organisational ecology".[4]

Fourthly, there will be a need to perceive the organisation design as a challenge to explore multiple choices between various forms of work organisation.   This involves the realisation that personnel activity may be redesigned so that it can, on the one hand, become responsive to the innovative culture and, on the other hand, become also an initiator of innovation by its own example to other segments of an organisation.

Fifthly, the advisory and staff functions will need to be perceived as essentially a system-based shared function where responsibility towards organisational objectives and commitment to employees' needs and expectations are an integrated task.   This is not to deny or denigrate the need for specialised knowledge among certain clusters of the employees, but it clearly shows the importance of a mutuality between roles and functions that leads to a converging commitment towards similarity of purpose.

Sixthly, the personnel function can no longer be a dumping ground for a broad array of activities that the organisation can allocate to the personnel department.[5] In other words, the personnel function will have to be consistently identified with the human resources field.

Lastly, innovation in organisations implies a reallocation of power.   While the formal sources of power are a reality and cannot be wished away, it must be recognised that there are informal sources of power as well, essentially non-hierarchical, and taking the two together, the personnel department will have to become a co-partner in the exercise of power.   In short, interdepartmental conflict will need to be replaced by interfunctional interdependence and co-operation, a development that becomes conceivable as the personnel function assumes the role of management of human resources.

3. Towards restructuring the
    personnel department

Herzberg believes that there is a need for the personnel department to be so organised as to respond to the management of hygiene factors and the management of motivator factors (extrinsic role and intrinsic role).[6] The essence of his proposal is presented in figure 1.

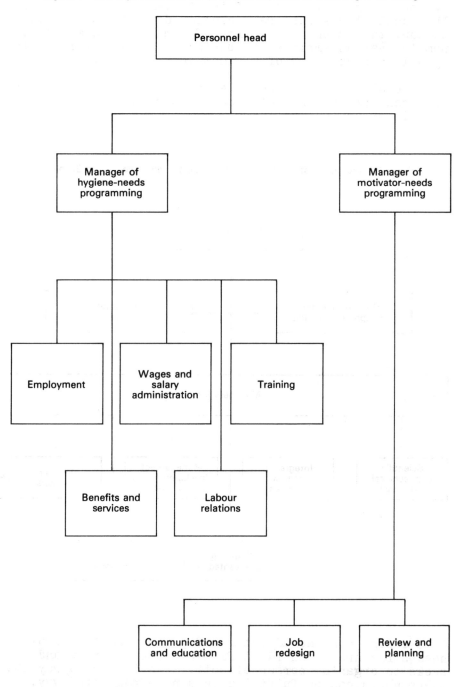

While there may be numerous criticisms of this
approach, there is one that is relevant to our discussion.
This dualistic structural solution does not take into
account the essential reality of human beings at work,
namely that an employee is basically a complex man with
dynamic ebb and flow of his motive structure.

Sokolik has utilised the insights of the market seg-
ment concept in restructuring the personnel function.[7]
This is presented in figure 2.

Figure 2 The organisation of the personnel department according to Sokolik

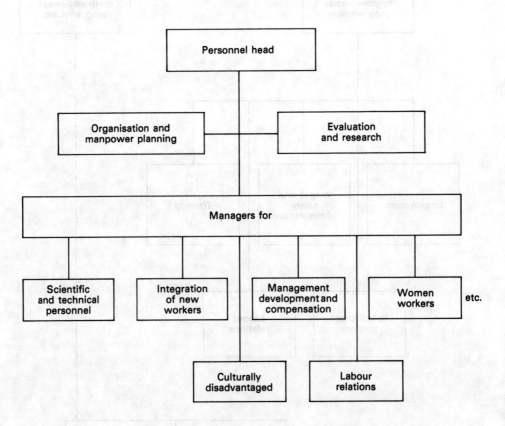

This design has the advantage of perceiving the total
need structure of an identifiable interest group and
seeks to organise personnel activities in such a way that
these needs can be fulfilled in a non-fragmented way.
The author also accepts the reality that these groups,
however, will have a high degree of interdependence.

A case study

In September 1976, in the Hardwar Heavy Electricals
Equipment Plant of Bharat Heavy Electricals Limited in
India, experiences with new forms of work organisation in
several production shops called for a reorientation in
the structure and functioning of the personnel department. The shop-floor workers had been organised in
semi-autonomous work groups with enlarged collective
responsibility for production tasks based on multiple
skills, on job learning and on the initial monitoring of
tasks, responsibilities and supervision. They became
somewhat uneasy about the lack of responsiveness in the
personnel and finance divisions to their grievances and
needs. It is not that the personnel department was apa-
thetic to the employees' individual problems, but with
new awareness, the shop-floor workers could see that,
while they could operate fairly successfully in a non-
hierarchical fashion, the response pattern in the personnel department was still of the typical bureaucratic
type. An employee from the shop floor with a grievance
about his leave salary and overtime payment had to run
from pillar to post because he had to deal with different
functionaries to get his problem resolved.

When this problem became the subject of open discussion, a task force of the personnel department devoted
itself to looking into its own operational organisation.
After some deliberation, the personnel division was
organised into three groups - one dealing with the personnel in plant operation and maintenance, the second
with the design, engineering and commercial groups and
the third with policy matters located in the office of
the Executive Director. The group that came to deal
with the largest number of workers involved in plant
operation and maintenance consisted of 22 persons
organised into three operating sub-groups - one dealing
with the problems of supervisory and clerical staff,
another group dealing with skilled workers and the third
dealing with semi-skilled and unskilled workers. The
functional division of work was thus replaced by a total
service package. However, in order to ensure that the
three groups functioning autonomously did not come to
conflicting decisions and policy recommendations, a
three-man co-ordinating team was set up to work closely
with the policy group on the one hand and the group
entrusted with the interest of the design, engineering
and commercial groups on the other. The structure that
emerged can be represented in a somewhat simple manner
in figure 3.

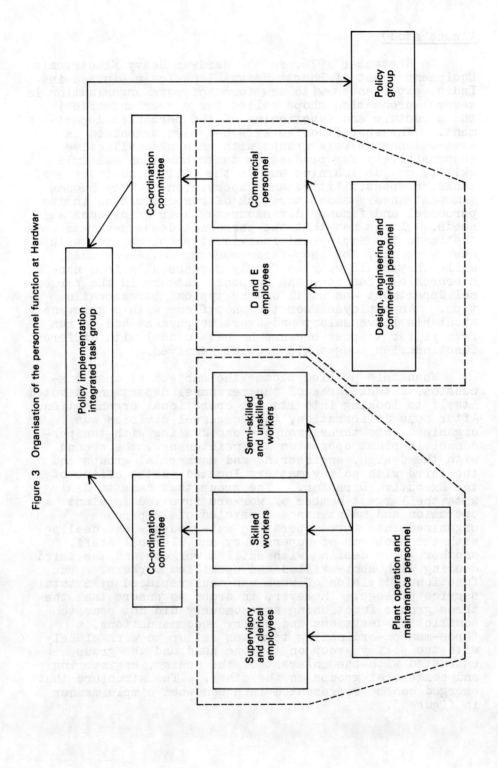

Figure 3   Organisation of the personnel function at Hardwar

Policy group

Co-ordination committee

Commercial personnel

D and E employees

Design, engineering and commercial personnel

Policy implementation integrated task group

Semi-skilled and unskilled workers

Skilled workers

Co-ordination committee

Supervisory and clerical employees

Plant operation and maintenance personnel

One defect in this design that needs to be mentioned is that training activities as a developmental function located in the training division were not yet integrated. They still come under the control of the production manager. While the experiment goes on stabilising itself, the training function may get attached to the personnel division. However, the working of the system indicates that at the clerical level in the personnel department a good deal of satisfaction has been expressed with the new system of working where variety, autonomy and meaningfulness of job have improved perceptibly. At the officers' level, however, there is still some doubt whether the functional specialisation would not be jeopardised by the creation of such integrated working groups.

This illustration is of particular significance because it has evolved in a developing country where the industrial culture, though not new, is still based on the traditional concept of work organisation. One interesting point is that the urge to develop this new form of work organisation in the personnel department has derived from the developments that took place on the shop floor. There has been a response strategy in the personnel department rather than initiative-based self-expression seeking to create a more meaningful work system. It is thus not surprising that the industrial engineering group, which has been involved from the beginning in the work redesign experiment, has not felt the need to develop interdependent relations with the personnel department. In other words, this illustration seeks to highlight the potential of developing new approaches to personnel work, but does not provide as satisfactory a solution to a complex problem as one would like to have.

4. The new role for the
    personnel department

The essential step will be to get away from the traditional industrial engineering approach or its counterpart in the office, known as the organisation and method approach, in manpower planning and deployment. It is not suggested that some of the techniques employed in these approaches are invalid or irrelevent. The basic thrust, however, is that the organisation design issue is, on the one hand, associated with certain basic values and concepts about human nature as mentioned in the earlier section and, on the other, contingent upon technological and related issues.

The concern for job specialisation and job simplification designed to ensure quality and reduce learning time will invariably lead to fragmented job structures and the application of the redundancy principle so far as the staffing pattern is concerned.[8] The dysfunction of this strategy is a powerful factor necessitating an active search for new forms of work organisation based on several of the socio-psychological forces that motivate employees to work.[9] By and large, the staffing pattern has been a close preserve of industrial engineers and production managers. In white-collar jobs, where the measurement problem is somewhat more diffuse, the line managers in charge of staff functions usually determine the staff strength, the hierarchy of levels and the deployment of persons on certain assumptions about requisite knowledge, skills and experience. Personnel functionaries do not usually figure at the design stage. Their entry into the scene occurs at a later stage of recruitment, selection induction and training.

It is suggested that a responsive personnel department in a culture of new forms of work organisation will need to be actively engaged from the beginning in the totality of tasks. However, to make meaningful contributions, personnel functionaries will have to appreciate the complex role that technology can play in determining the staffing pattern. The assumption that technology is supreme and determines the character of staffing is to be replaced by a more realistic assumption that the "properties" of technology and the "properties" of the social system can be jointly optimised in alternative ways.

Another important point is that "optimisation" is also a function of human behaviour determined by the size of the work setting. Barker has shown that the smaller the number of persons involved in a task system (however, there is a cut-off point below which the logic will not operate), the greater is the likelihood that the persons will structure themselves to carry out the totality of tasks and in the process seek to find ways of giving up "inappropriate" roles.[10] Vroom has gone further, to indicate that larger work groups tend to favour authoritarian leadership, for want of co-ordination among other factors, and that larger firms have a tendency to become too stable, rigid and resistant to change in an ever-changing environment.[11] Thus there is something to be said in favour of smaller groups in the allocation of work roles.

Recruitment is yet another function, conceivable in terms of job descriptions and identification of the potential labour market, that can offer the types of employees required. While one cannot set out rules of universal application, certain basic premises must be looked into. The tendency to secure the services of "finished products" is high. However, what needs to be appreciated is that for each job there are some essential personality variables that may respond to intrinsic character. Information received about candidates can, at most, act as a negative mechanism for rejection; it cannot provide adequate information about the positive elements that are critical to selection purpose. Another aspect refers to the disadvantaged groups seeking employment in a society. A uniform yardstick of selection will work against them. A basic faith that continuing learning is practicable in an organisation and that efforts can be initiated to bring persons of different capabilities up to standard through involvement in the work process can result in various alternative approaches to the problem. This problem is perhaps more acute in developing countries, where regional imbalances in development have resulted in the continuous neglect of certain sections of the population in the matter of recruitment. These include persons of varying cultural background, such as migrant workers, women and in India the lower castes and members of tribes.

We can now identify some of the alternative approaches to the problem of manpower planning and the effective utilisation of human resources:

(i) There must be a participative planning of manpower needs. Manpower planning is not necessarily a specialised job; it is conceivable that personnel functionaries, industrial engineers, trade union leaders and the workers concerned may be able to plan together the design of the social system of work allowing an optimum solution with a new meaning and providing an opportunity for overcoming redundancy on the one hand and rejecting alienation on the other.

(ii) In the matter of recruitment and selection, the practice of the Kalmar factory of Volvo provides another possibility. When a vacancy in a work group is reported to the personnel department, it circulates a note in the local community and the candidates are called in to inter-act with the work group of which the supervisor is a member and, on the basis of this inter-action, selection takes place. Experience shows this method to have two major advantages. Once the workers themselves are actively involved in the selection process, they can assess their potential colleagues on the basis of the key requirements of the job. Secondly, they take upon themselves the responsibility of integrating the new members into their team.

It is true that in a country like Sweden, where unemployment is not a serious problem, such a scheme may work satisfactorily in a small community like that of Kalmar. In a developing country, however, this may not be so. On the other hand, there is a future for the basic principle of participation as a process of selection that can be extended to a group of work colleagues of reasonable size if not to the entire work team.

(iii) In respect of socially and economically disadvantaged groups including migrant labour, recruitment, selection and induction need to be conceived and planned so as to provide congenial work and human environment for these persons. Here too, instead of entirely depending on the knowledge of the experts and specialists, a participative forum can be created where workers can actively take interest in integrating these special groups into the work and the community systems. This role will add a new dimension to the quality of life of the existing workforce.

(iv) With regard to women employees, there is a need to recognise their special need to harmonise their family responsibilities and the urge to become socially relevant through involvement in a meaningful work process. Special rules with provision for flexibility will be required to deal with this kind of problem.

In conclusion, then, we may emphasise the desirability of a pluralistic interest-group-oriented personnel policy where there will be a high premium on participation and adaptive planning.

5. The new role in continuing education for employees

An idea gaining ground is that any type of work system should be learning-oriented and any type of learning system should be work-oriented. In other words, learning and working are to be perceived in a practical relation, each enlarging the frontier of the other. This will lead to a departure from the conception of training that has taken traditional roots in what Fromm calls the "pathology of normalcy".[12] Training has been perceived essentially as an amalgam of two processes, occupational socialisation and organisational socialisation.

Training as a function of the work process

New forms of work organisation lead to a departure from this orientation. Not only the content of training, but also the processes involved in training need redefinition. The accent is placed more and more on a culture of continuing education. Emery has identified the mission of this continuing education in three dimensions:[13]

(i)   to identify the leading elements of a social system in which radical new types of learning are required for the guidance of social practice;

(ii) to create social settings in which the actors are enabled to identify whatever they need to learn;

(iii) to help the learners to understand how they can create in their own organisations the conditions of the culture of learning they are to learn.

At one level the cognitive map for learning dynamics can be presented in a framework modifying the model used by Kolb and his associates.[14] See figure 4. We shall provide three examples to show how this dynamics can operate outside the framework of the traditional concept of training.

(a) In the Hardwar plant of Bharat Heavy Electricals Limited in India, the two condenser fabrication production shops became concerned in actively redesigning their work system in 1975. In two groups there were 25 workmen belonging to different trades (welders, fitters, crane operators, fettlers, etc.). Through a process of active planning, carried out with the supervisors, the groups not only redefined their task objective but also reorganised themselves into small work teams. They soon discovered that, in order to make the teams autonomous in functioning, the trade-based work pattern had to be replaced by a system in which they learnt each other's trade with a view to creating meaningful interdependence and inter-linkage among the members of the team. The workers themselves, while involved in the work process, started working with other workers having different trades and skills with a view to learning these. At times they felt the need for theoretical inputs, such as an interpretation of the drawings, in order to fulfil a task within the allowed tolerances. In such situations, they called on the services of their supervisors and instructors from the training institute.

Over a period of one year, trade "redundancy" was
created within the groups, so much so that, whereas
previously there had been one crane operator in each
group, after a year a number of other workers with
different designations mastered the art of working
overhead cranes.   Similarly, the crane operators
acquired some of the skills traditionally those of
fitters and welders.   Gradually, they moved further
and started involving themselves in production
scheduling and planning.   Their cognitive map of
the total task system in the group underwent a major
change in the process.   A systemic approach to
the problem replaced the traditional concept of one
man, one job.

Figure 4   A cognitive map of learning dynamics

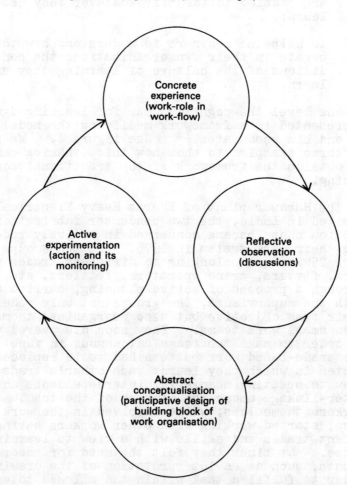

This framework calls for the initiation of certain processes implicit in the concept of participative
design.

(b) In the postal service in India,* when the delivery postman, the sorter postman and the clerks dealing with records of accountable items (registered letters, money orders, insured covers, etc.) formed themselves into an integrated delivery group, it was found that the total time spent in sorting operations and the house-to-house delivery of mail was curtailed by about an hour. Interdependence within the group made it possible to complete the work at a faster pace without creating any pressure on its members.

At the same time it was known that there was a perpetual shortage of staff in the post offices because year after year the reserve quota for promotion to the grade of counter clerk was not filled, the postmen being unable to pass the departmental examination. The reason was that the tests were essentially oriented towards the practical problems met by counter clerks, to which the postmen were not exposed.

The participative design spirit came to the rescue and it was planned that the postmen could very well use their free hour preparing themselves for the tests, for which the counter clerks could train them. So, within the workplace itself, a culture of learning was created in a more functional way with neither extra cost to the postal system nor the allocation of any extra time to this task by employees. The new work system design could create not only the opportunities but also the motivation for undertaking this continuing learning process within the work process itself.

(c) In the 1960s, M. Scott Myers reported a similar experience, in which artisans who were new entrants in Texas Instruments were initially exposed to the basic production functions in the factory and then asked to help to redesign their own training programmes with active support from the instructors. The new programme for classroom learning was occasionally monitored by testing out the ongoing learning in an actual work situation. As a result, the training period could be shortened and the quality of learning - in knowledge and in skill - was found to have improved.

---

* See also The Case Study at the end of Chapter 6.

These illustrations lead to the conclusion that it is possible for individual employees to work out their course for the acquisition of knowledge and skills, provided that there is a group basis for experimentation and that organisational support is made available to them.

This model of working-learning as an integrated process is a departure from the traditional pattern of classroom learning, which is the option of traditional personnel departments. This design, however, does not imply that classroom learning is redundant. What it essentially signifies is a redefinition of the learning model. Innovative ways can be devised and this is possible if the personnel department, which is usually entrusted with the training function, adapts itself to the new culture. For a developing country in particular, this approach is likely to be a low-cost training package. Its major effect lies in the strengthening of democratic values in training activities irrespective of the stage of industrial development. Continuing education is but a logical extension of the democratisation process.

Counselling as a learning process

The learning process is essentially a helping process but the character of the helping role is what is relevant here. The notion that a learner is a receptacle into which knowledge has to be poured by the knowledgeable also denotes a helping process, but its dynamics are dichotomous - one party receives help and the other party renders help. This conception of helping requires to be replaced by a new conception of counselling in terms of a process based on dialogue. This process, as explained by Freire, implies that the learner and the trainer are both active subjects jointly and collaboratively exploring an object (the subject-matter of the learning).[15] According to this conception, the distinction between the two gets blurred and there is an explicit assumption that both parties can contribute to the exploration of a problem or the mastering of a new art or the pursuit of a new line of knowledge.

For the personnel functionaries to play this kind of role would mean, firstly, a redefinition of the objective of training and, secondly, an exercise of empathic skills and an attitude of "being with the learners" in exploring the range of alternatives instead of setting out a predetermined course or goal for them. This dynamic relation essentially implies that the helper and the receiver, in particular the helper, will have to perceive the structure of the learning relation in terms of social power rather than personal power, affiliation need and a

128

joint optimisation of achievement need. The motives and
the self-esteem of the personnel man cast in a training
role are some of the key factors here. The realisation
that the receiver of training is essentially a contributor
to the training situation is the key to redefining his
motive-structure and to his acquiring high self-esteem by
getting engaged in an active learning-searching process.

By and large, then, the adult learning process in a
new form of work organisation is a radical departure from
the university model of learning. Problem-solving
skills based on the acquisition of relevant knowledge
are necessary. But the new approach goes a step further
through this joint learning process.

6. The new role of career planning

Career planning under new forms of work organisation
is linked with the staffing pattern and the learning culture at one end and the reward system at the other. In
that sense, career planning is a bridge between the two
ends.

Some key parameters in the gamut of career planning
are the following:

(i) a balance between adult socialisation and the
process of innovation;

(ii) the individual's role in career determination;

(iii) the cadre concept, the quota system and promotion policy;

(iv) the concept of the specialist role and the
preservation of expertise;

(v) organisation culture.

Before we proceed any further, a comment seems to be
in order. In recent years, a good deal of research and
thought have been devoted to career planning issues for
scientists and managers, but very little has been done in
respect of blue-collar and office employees. The same
trends are present in developing countries. At the
instance of top management, personnel functionaries
devote time to career planning, cadre management and promotion opportunities linked with management development
in respect of young professional entrants and middle-
level managers. In respect of the lower level employees,
the issue comes through the process of union-management

bargaining, in which career planning finds expression in promotion to higher grades, monetary rewards and techno-logical pressure, leading to the retraining of the work-force for redeployment to other jobs. A systematic planning process being absent, the trade union presses the issue and, depending on the exigencies of the situa-tion, some kind of compromise solutions are reached.

In respect of new forms of work organisation, one significant aspect is that the more successful cases of experimentation have evolved from the bottom up, although there are a limited number of cases of top-down, centre-down and centre-out approaches.* If the bottom-up approach is the commonest, then suitable career planning for the lower levels of employees becomes important in an organisation; however, it does not preclude the need for an integrated approach to career planning involving various categories of employees.

A balance between adult socialisation and the process of innovation

The movement of persons vertically (rank or level concept), radially (centrality concept) and circumferen-tially (movement-across-the-function concept) depends upon the structural priorities of the organisation and also on the concept of boundaries - the degree of permea-bility and the filtering process.[16] These properties of structure and boundaries are to a great extent determined by the degree of influence that an organisation can exert upon an individual. This is basically an adult sociali-sation process. If there is too much of it, the conform-ism will become a culture and in such a situation the spirit of innovation may get blunted. There is, there-fore, a need to encourage a spirit of questioning, search for alternative choices and ability to dialogue on prob-lems. The more structured an organisation is and the more specific and bounded its roles are, the less are the chances that an innovative culture will be generated.

The individual's role in career determination

Here, it is essentially a question of how far an individual sees himself as an "actor" as opposed to a "pawn". The actor role does not necessarily mean a spirit of rugged independence or individualism but rather the ability to develop a stable self-concept that can seek to carry out reality testing in the context of one's

---

* See Chapter 6.

own life goals.[17]   In new forms of work organisation, where groups develop job designs and work roles, these can generate ideas for career prospects.   In such a situation, the actor becomes an interdependent entity in a network of persons without losing his identity.   A "pawn" on the other hand, will surrender himself to external forces and either depend on the decision-makers of the organisation to plan for him or on what his trade union is capable of delivering to him.

At the individual level, there is yet another psychodynamic element with an interplay between the conscious and the unconscious.[18]   That there are unconscious emotional forces operating within an individual is an undeniable fact of life whose complexity is not easy to resolve by organisational devices.   On the other hand, a congenial work group setting can provide opportunities for self-exploration, which can lead to self-disclosure and self-illumination through a helpful and insightful feedback from colleagues and so to a process of resolving unconscious conflicts.

The cadre concept, the quota system and promotion policy

The functional concept of organisation has brought into existence different cadres, either on the basis of specialisation of knowledge (for example, R and D scientists) or on the basis of organisational needs (maintenance engineers, customs service, postal service, etc.). The traditional approach, which is still predominant, is that the members of a cadre look forward to their career planning within the cadre, although at the higher reaches of an organisation the concept of general management may lead to a quota system in which a certain percentage of posts are reserved for different cadres including some for direct recruits and promotees from below.   A time-bound promotion policy is very often the result of such an approach, although level-jumping on the basis of out-standing performances reflected in appraisal systems is more usual.

In new forms of work organisation, this concept clashes with the expectations of employees and the needs of the job.   In an integrated multi-skilled work group, as in the Hardwar unit of Bharat Heavy Electricals Limited, it has been found that unskilled and semi-skilled workers do acquire skills in other trades and that a time-bound promotion policy as a way of planning their career then acts as a demotivating factor for them. The policy came under attack by the employees concerned. In the interest of the equity principle throughout the organisation, the management is equally reluctant to

develop alternative policies for these experimental
groups and at times their fear of reactions from
traditional work groups is justified. Yet organisational innovation will call for a change in the policy
and this is where imaginative support from the trade
unions is necessary.

The concept of the specialist role
and the preservation of expertise

It is appreciated that there are highly specialised
jobs in which the nature of the challenge in the job
itself can provide a high degree of motivation for the
employees concerned. These employees may not be
interested in changing their role across the functions
nor are they likely to be too much interested in moving
to general management positions. In their cases, career
planning would take a different shape. Provision for
growth in the job with the ability to manage more and
more of the job contents at their discretion might act as
a career incentive, provided that the organisation reward
structure was flexible enough to recognise their contributions in a worth-while way. Highly skilled workers
and middle to higher level specialists, particularly
R and D scientists, may thus be governed by a career
planning logic distinct from that applying to unskilled
workers and general purpose supervisory and managerial
cadres.

Organisation culture

The effective realisation of the elements mentioned
above will depend upon the type of culture that an
organisation has. If the organisation looks upon new
forms of work systems as essentially a way of providing
efficient management for technology and the products of
technology, then career planning is likely to follow the
more traditional forms. If, on the other hand, the
people at work acquire a high degree of saliency, the
organisation culture will permit the development of systems encouraging participative design in career planning.
There are examples to show that the provision of some
freedom for the employees to design the career structure
in relation to new work systems has been fruitful. A
culture of continuing education, non-hierarchical autonomous group working with extended boundaries and a high
degree of permeability across the work boundaries is what
is called for.

The ideas discussed above can be presented in the
form of a diagram: see figure 5.

The personnel functionaries' role in this framework
is to inter-act with the various interest groups in an
organisation and then plan for the successive steps
indicated in figure 5, bearing in mind that there is no
one answer to career planning and promotion prospects.

Firstly, the future traditionally sought after today
consists in moving up in grade, or, failing that, moving
towards successively higher pay scales without significant changes in jobs or roles, which leads to too many
levels of overlapping pay scales. The result is more
outlay per employee than his commensurate contribution is
likely to provide in the fulfilment of the tasks of the
organisation. This psychological blockage of the personnel man and of the management will need to be replaced
by the clear realisation that career planning not only is
a matter of incremental financial outlay, but has other
components as well, such as the growth and development of
employees in a job or in a cluster of jobs, which can
lead to an increasing contribution to the tasks of the
organisation. For some classes of employees such as
specialists, it may become a more individualistic
approach, while for others it may emanate from group
norms and a group-sanctioned solution.

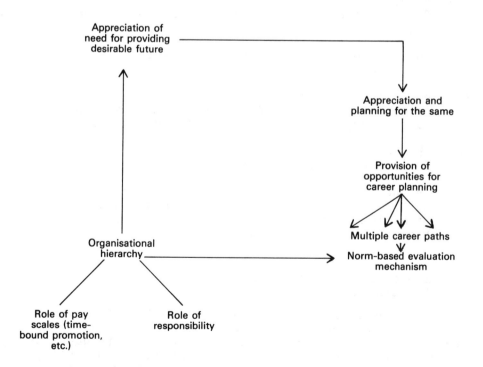

Secondly, the mid-career crisis problem, as reflected in the Peter principle, is an issue that calls for two types of approach. The counselling role of helping the persons concerned to manage their disappointments in a productive way by searching for alternatives, which may include lateral movement to another job or even exit from an organisation for the taking up of responsibilities meeting certain other needs (for example, more freedom to spend time with the family and be placed in a socially relevant community group) can become a new dimension to the personnel function.

Thirdly, the provision of opportunities for overcoming obsolescence in the employees' knowledge which may include involvement in temporary project teams, re-entry into the education system for upgrading knowledge and skills and so on, is also something to add to the personnel function. Participative design and search-type adaptive planning can surely open up opportunities to deal with lower level dead-end jobs.

Fourthly, it will be necessary to develop an appraisal system including multiple criteria, at least three of which are critical:

(a) specific task performance with provision for frequent feedback and support from above when required;

(b) concrete evidence of active interest in developing the subordinates;

(c) concrete evidence of offering help and co-operation to colleagues across functional areas and others who have to depend on the person as a resource.

The development of multiple criteria is not enough. The evaluation mechanism will have to be open enough for the persons concerned to know where they stand in their career structure and for their colleagues to become aware of the comparative picture in which promotion on the basis of performance is likely to become an acceptable culture.

7. The role in an evolving
   reward system

A reward system in an organisational setting is a product of numerous variables. Some of these variables are the socio-economic system of the society in question, the general standard of living and the income per head, levels of employment and the role of the State in the provision of social benefits for the population. The stage of economic development of a country and the macro-planning process are also relevant. So are the structure and the role of the trade union movement.

Another significant element is the interplay between work-related issues and interest-related issues in the context of a national framework that may provide flexibility for individual organisations and conformity to certain national norms.

In an open-system democratic form of society, whether in a developing country or in a developed country, union-management culture usually gives a definitive form to the reward system. It usually refers to <u>extrinsic rewards</u>. On the other hand, new forms of work organisation have also been motivated by a concern for the quality of working life with a view to fulfilling certain basic social and psychological needs that seek to motivate people to work, and so provide <u>intrinsic rewards</u>. To take one aspect by way of illustration, autonomous group functioning can open up a range of opportunities for the employees, both as individuals and as members of a work team, of fulfilling certain non-material satisfactions in their work setting. Instead of feeling that as employees they are playing an instrumental role in subserving the demands of technology, they may experience a sense of satisfaction so far as they can control the operation of technology. This is where an active planning process is to be created by an organisation system, a process in which the personnel functionaries will have to use their insight about a variety of intrinsic job satisfaction elements. Herzberg's concept of job enrichment need not be perceived as an exclusive response to the needs. Group-based intrinsic rewards can also become a fruitful source of satisfaction. As a matter of fact, there are instances where, despite the structural limitation on extending material rewards to employees, as in the postal system in India, the post office employees continued with their experiments at Simla and Delhi because of the freedom that the new structure afforded them and the feeling of well-being that they experienced in controlling the technology of the work system.

Material rewards[*]

Material rewards are, however, equally relevant. After all, the industrial system is based on the utilitarian concept of an exchange between inducements and

---

[*] Chapter 5 deals with this issue in more detail.

contributions and the consumerism culture is there to
remind the employees that material benefits are a major
source of work motivation. The economic principle
dominates the scene even when an effort is made through
participative design to restructure the work system.
Directly or indirectly, managements are concerned with
productivity gains and so the employees' response to a
change in their work habit and work culture will be to
ask for adequate compensation. There is also the fear
of redundancy among employees and the shrinkage of the
employment potential in a free enterprise system. Where
there are genuine reasons to fear redundancy,
the material reward structure will include an additional
component of security of employment, irrespective of the
state-planned social security benefit schemes, however
elaborate they may be. If the history of industrial
relations in an organisation is riddled with conflict
situations and power-based confrontation, the propensity
to secure additional material benefits for participation
in new forms of work organisation will be stronger.

That is one reason why, with a strong enduring culture of collaborative relations between trade unions and
managements in the Scandinavian countries, trade union
agreement was obtained for starting with experimental
projects.

The experience of the Christiana Spigerverk wire-
drawing mill in Norway offers an interesting insight into
the material reward scheme. A time came during the
later phases of the experiment when the incentive earnings of the experimental work groups gave rise to a
stalemate situation since the national agreements between
the Association of Employers and the Federation of
Employees could not permit the sharing of productivity
gains without repercussions on other groups of employees.
Another constraining factor was that the sharing of
productivity gains could have brought about a disruption
of status payment relations in the industry, wire-drawers
having the possibility of earning as much as the top
steel furnace workers. A somewhat similar problem arose
in the Hardwar Heavy Electrical Equipment Plant in India.
On top of the time-rate pay scale, members of the experimental work groups enjoyed a group reward scheme, which
was based on performance over the historically predetermined production standards. This particular scheme
was also operated for the non-experimental work groups,
but the major difference appeared when the tradition of
extra pay for overtime was eliminated in the experimental
work groups because of an effective group functioning
that was absent from the non-experimental work groups.
There were instances where non-experimental work group
members were earning more at the end of a month through
overtime pay, and this created resentment amongst the

members of the experimental groups, whose earnings truly reflected the productive effort that they were putting into their work. Another difficulty arose in respect of the closed-panel fabrication experimental group, where it was discovered that, despite effective group working, the reward scheme was not remunerative enough because frequent design changes made by the designers nullified the work that had been put in by members of the experimental group, where it was discovered that, despite effective group working, the reward scheme was not remunerative enough because frequent design changes made by the designers nullified the work that had been put in by members of the experimental group. The management was somewhat reluctant to modify the scheme for this group only, since it was uncertain what effect this would have on other work groups.

Yet another problem that can often arise, is the inability to develop equitable criteria for the distribution of the total incentive earnings of the group, at least in the initial phase. An unskilled worker who put in additional effort to acquire new skills while at work might get a quantum of incentive bonus proportionate to his basic salary while another worker with less effort might earn more because his basic pay was higher. After all, a team does not become a "psychological" group in a short time simply because a work team has been created, even on a voluntary basis.

A guaranteed minimum wage, an assurance that redundant workers would not be thrown out of employment and the reward structure conceived as a package deal for the experimental period rather than as an established pattern would perhaps be a practical way of dealing with this problem. There should also be an additional provision for the guaranteed wage where new experiments might lead to an initial setback to production and productivity. These tasks have to be jointly undertaken by personal functionaries, industrial engineers, production managers and the production planning and control group. The concept of direct and indirect work (production versus maintenance function) and blue-collar and white-collar work in an experimental group cannot be maintained on traditional lines. This is where personnel people will have to accept the logic of the new situation, which, experience indicates, can be applied more easily to industrial engineers and production managers.

To sum up, in designing the extrinsic reward structure, the personnel functionaries will need to develop these approaches:

(a) to design the reward structure in a participative manner with the active involvement of industrial engineers, operating managers and trade unions;

(b) the avoidance of too many layers of pay scales along with elaborate hierarchical structures;

(c) incentive systems should be carefully worked out. The piece-rate system does not easily fit into autonomous group functioning. An imaginative balance of group incentives, flexi-hours, time off for learning opportunities, the discouragement of overtime, the prospect of Scanlon type plans, etc., may have to be attempted;

(d) though standard data and other methods may have to be utilised in deciding on production norms, these should be carried out in a participative manner - not only as an expert-group exercise;

(e) the traditional distinction between direct and indirect work is often questionable in a culture of "collective work";

(f) career planning as a reward system should take into account multi-skilling, group responsibility and other forms of challenge that the groups have taken upon themselves;

(g) job separation on account of new forms of work organisation has to be guarded against;

(h) the administration of the reward system should be non-bureaucratic and not too complicated.

8. Seeking trade union support

There are instances where it has been alleged, with some justification, that certain corporations have taken the initiative in establishing new forms of work organisation because they could sense that this would either help to keep the trade unions at a distance or at least weaken the trade union movement. There are allegations that the purpose of Texas Instruments, Polaroid, Proctor and Gamble and General Foods in the United States in favouring the work restructuring philosophy was to keep their plants non-unionised.[19, 20]

Without going into the specific situation of these and similar companies, the general point is that new forms of work organisation cannot be successfully initiated and stabilised without trade union support and, ideally, trade union participation. In fact, with imaginative management leadership, it is the experience in the Indian postal system, the Bolivar Project in the United States and the Hardwar plant of BHEL, that it is possible to draw initial critical support from the trade union leaders. Their active involvement in the experiment could forestall many an awkward situation and possible stalemate.

Certain broad conclusions concerning personnel implication in the new forms of work organisation can be drawn from the experiences of different countries:

(i) With a strong politically oriented trade union movement, the initial dialogue to explore the possibility of alternative forms of work organisation must take place at two levels: top management, with national or regional level trade union leaders; and the personnel functionaries, with the plant-based trade union leaders. Once the broad parameters are worked out even for time-bound experimental projects, more detailed participative discussions can take place between the shop-floor managers and the shop-floor trade union leaders. It may be desirable to create a joint monitoring group to oversee the progress of the project. Social scientists did not form a prominent third party in Sweden, but they did in Norway, England, France, Holland and Italy. The Indian experience has been the same, particularly because of the comparative inexperience of the management in developing an appropriate strategy to initiate the projects.

(ii) It may be worth while to develop two forums - either on parallel lines or with common membership - to deal with work-related issues (work redesign projects) and interest-related issues, so that they can complement each other. By and large, experience has been reasonably satisfactory where a multiplicity of trade unions is an additional factor. These two forums can work more satisfactorily if the personnel men get engaged in the projects actively, for otherwise their concern will be more with the resolution of interest-related issues without an adequate understanding of or insight into work-related issues.

(iii) Experience inside organisations of a strategy for evolving new forms of work organisation is rare. By and large, a step-by-step

139

approach has so far been adopted. One
handicap with this approach is that it
creates constraints in evolving the reward
structure, particularly of the extrinsic
kind, for selective groups, since it is
likely to disrupt the equity of monetary
rewards throughout the organisation. A
payment structure cannot be modified easily
to suit the functional requirements of the
experimental groups. Trade unions themselves would hesitate to take the risk.

There is thus a need for further exploration
of the project initiation strategy so that
several experimental sites can begin simultaneously, provided that an adequate number
of motivated managers, personnel men and
trade union officials are available for
the projects:

(iv) Inevitably, the time lag between the ongoing
success of an experiment and the modification
of the reward structure has to be reduced.
Unless this is done, there is bound to be
discontent. In the Hardwar plant, it took
more than a year to develop even a once-only
symbolic reward for the members of the
experimental groups in recognition of the
good work that they have been able to accom-
plish. It was feared that this reward might
cause discontent in other worksites. The
personnel people will have to assess situations and eventualities and act in time to
deal with these undesirable consequences by
developing positive schemes to neutralise
them.

It may be worth while to reflect on the dynamic
character of human motivation in a work situation. Odaka
has been able to identify five types of workers' response
to the relative importance of work and leisure.[21] This
situation may not be peculiar to Japan. At the same
time, one may reflect[22] on an interesting development in
the Bolivar Project. Here, facilitated by the direct
involvement of the workers and trade unions in redesigning the work system, the workers responded to
extra free time made available through the productivity
gains by utilising it at the worksite to upgrade their
work-related knowledge and skills as a positive step
towards improving their careers. Under normal circumstances, that is, in the absence of a participative redesign of the work system, workers might have used the
free time on traditional forms of leisure time
activities.

9. The new role in an evolving industrial relations system

The industrial relations system is composed of two basic elements:

(a) Certain rules, regulations, norms and guidelines, deriving from the machinery of the State or the joint efforts of trade unions and management or both, to regulate the relations between an employer and his employees at one level and between an employer and a trade union at another. The regulatory mechanisms may also include intervention in various forms by a third party.

(b) An inter-group dynamics involving two power groups located in a situation where the inter-action is founded on the representative roles of the two parties. Neither party is "fully sovereign", for each only represents its constituency.

Historically, with the rise of the trade union movement, the prerogatives of management have undergone a change. The "executive role" of management has remained, though confined to the broad spectrum of work-related issues, while the interest-related issues have become the subject of the industrial relations system.

In socialist countries, where the party in power incorporates the trade union movement within its over-all policy control, the dualistic role of interest-related issues and work-related issues does not exist to any significant extent, because an enterprise has to operate within the over-all framework of state policy. In market-economy countries, however, two trends have emerged. In some of them, in particular the Scandinavian countries, the political and cultural tradition resulting in the social homogeneity of the population has brought about collaborative relations between trade unions and management. There is thus some degree of permeability between work-related issues and interest-related issues. In most countries, the dichotomous character of the two sets of issues has been maintained.

Where the dichotomy has been maintained, the industrial relations system has assumed the character of a distributive bargaining culture, with the two parties involved in a joint decision-making process to resolve conflicts of interest on the premise that the limited resources are to be shared in a manner that should not be more favourable to one party than to the other. At an extreme, it may take the form of a zerosum game resulting in stalemate, overt conflict, industrial action and counteraction and the development of acrimonious relations.

The other possibility is an integrative bargaining system in which a conflict situation is perceived as a problem to be subjected to joint exploration leading to concrete decisions. "This is closely related to what game theorists call the varying-sum game".[23]

The one process element involved in the evolution of either system is the way the attitudes of the two parties are structured, including each party's perception of the other and an appreciation of each other's strengths and weaknesses. Trust and mistrust, the past history of inter-group relations and the orientation of leadership of the power spectrum are some of the variables that determine the attitudinal structure. The other relevant process element is the intra-organisational dynamics. The processes going on within each group to balance the conflicting interests, the power equation and the manner of reaching compromises, as behind the scene operations, will be reflected in the type of industrial relations system that emerges. These ideas can be presented in the form of a diagram:[24] see figure 6.

Figure 6   Types of bargaining relations

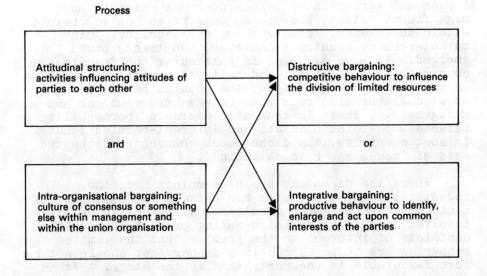

Process

Attitudinal structuring:
activities influencing attitudes of parties to each other

Districtive bargaining:
competitive behaviour to influence the division of limited resources

and

or

Intra-organisational bargaining:
culture of consensus or something else within management and within the union organisation

Integrative bargaining:
productive behaviour to identify, enlarge and act upon common interests of the parties

New forms of work organisation are based on a constructive accommodation process between the two parties.
There is thus a prospect of an interesting dynamics based
on integrative bargaining relations. From another point
of view, industrial democracy experiments can gradually
bring about a shift from a distributive bargaining
orientation to an integrative bargaining orientation.
Various experimental projects in the United Kingdom show
that once the initial breakthrough is obtained, through
a process of acquiescence by the trade unions in the experiments, the success experienced with new forms of
work organisation have a positive influence on the bargaining relations in a society where conflict has been
more prominent than co-operation. No doubt there have
been certain setbacks in Shell Refineries in the United
Kingdom and in other organisations involved in work redesign experiments, but this has been caused primarily
by the adverse economic situations that have developed
in England in recent years and the resultant retrench-
ment of the workforce. In such a situation, the trade
unions have been forced to withdraw their support from
work redesign experiments because their primary concern
is to protect the interests of their constituents.

Experiences in India show that, although at the
national level concern with new forms of work organisation is still undeveloped and receiving low priority
from the national trade union leaders and the employers'
organisations, at the micro level the initiative taken by
responsive managements has been met in a positive fashion
by the trade union leaders of enterprises. As in Norway
and Sweden, no national policy has been evolved in
support of industrial democracy, but a series of local-
level experiments has been undertaken and the industrial
relations culture has been influenced by integrative
bargaining principles.

In the Australian situation, where union-management
relations have been more or less similar to those of the
United Kingdom, certain enterprise-level experiments and
the urge of rank-and-file workers to experience democratic values in their work setting have brought about a
change in the orientation of national trade union leaders,
who came out with a positive policy statement on industrial democracy in the annual convention of the Australian Council of Trade Unions in 1977. Discussing the
Norwegian experience, Qvale[25] pointed out that the
success of grassroots experiments has not brought about
a commensurate democratisation process in the structure
and functioning of the national trade union movement and
the employers' organisations. They have remained bureaucratic and hierarchic in their culture, though at the
grassroots level non-hierarchical forms of work organisation have been experimented upon successfully.

One aspect of industrial relations that could play
a role complementary to that of industrial democracy
would be a reorientation by management of its attitudes
to trade unions and the development of an internal mechanism in which the dysfunctions of power-oriented bargaining could be avoided. Essentially, the personnel function has the responsibility of helping management in
developing appropriate strategies to deal with trade
unions.

To develop an alternative approach, the personnel
functionaries will need to attach significance to attitudinal structuring and intra-organisational bargaining
dynamics in a different way. It is possible to utilise
the psychological gains derived from the opportunities
offered by new forms of work organisation to improve the
quality of industrial relations. To that extent, new
forms of work organisation will provide an additional
positive element in restructuring the industrial relations system. The social reality and relevance of new
forms of work organisation may lead to a new form of
social ideology in industrial relations.

10. A change agent role for personnel functionaries

Our approach in looking at the personnel function
so far, is that the personnel role will need to be
reoriented in the context of alternative organisation
designs.

This brings us first to the issue of the change
agent role of personnel functionaries. Lewin's dictum
"if you want to understand something, try to change it",
is perhaps a meaningful definition of the change agent
role. However, this role can be misunderstood, if not
abused. In the first place, a change agent may develop
a tendency "to play God" by adopting intervention strategies that may be manipulative in nature. Secondly, and
related to the first issue, comes the concept of values.
No social change intervention is value-free. In fact,
an uncritical over-commitment to an objective or a
mission may lead to a change strategy with unintended
consequences for others. Unless the·values or the
ideals of the change agent are explicit, not as a part of
an "espoused theory" but as theory-in-use,[26] truly
reflecting actual behaviour, a change agent can become an
unconscious manipulative operator. The danger is all
the more real as personnel functionaries are accustomed
to active involvement in the power game vis-à-vis union-
management transactional relations. It is therefore
desirable that these dangers and other likely pitfalls
should be borne in mind.

Though there are a variety of roles that it is desirable, even necessary, for a personnel man to acquire in a new organisation design system, we shall highlight four elements:

(a) The non-hierarchical influence

In a hierarchical organisation system, there are, in broad power-profile terms, certain unequal forms of power, namely, sanction power, formal power, referent power and expert power. There are four levelling forms of power, namely persuasion power, influence upwards, influence downwards and professional skill. One conclusion of Mulder's research,[27] is that the greater the power distance is, the greater is the likelihood that "powerless" will find it difficult to engage themselves meaningfully in a participative process. In negative terms, they will tend to resist the influence of the "powerful" by various means. The implication of this analysis is that the personnel man will need to perceive himself, in his change agent role, as one utilising the levelling forms of power. In a participative culture, the levelling forms of power will not stand in the way of his contribution based on expertise.

Yet another aspect of power dynamics is the cultural profile of an organisation.[28] It is conceivable that power orientation and role orientation as a combination in the culture of an organisation are likely to contribute to a non-equal power style. The change agent role of the personnel man will require a genuine appreciation of this dynamics, and unfreezing from a non-equal power orientation to a levelling-type influence relation. Its implications are threefold: (1) "non-power" relations within the personnel department itself; (2) "non-power" relations with other management groups and staff functions; (3) "non-power" relations with trade union leaders and experimental work groups.

(b) The collaborative norm-setting role

Another role is that of internalising the collaborative spirit as a shared norm. Apart from complex personality variables that may facilitate the derivation of such an orientation from the experiences of early childhood (Erikson's epigenetic growth model throws light on this,[29] a commitment to organisational ideals and purposes, with adequate flexibility and adaptability in the planning and implementation processes of the organisation can also create a collaborative culture. A matrix form of organisation design is an example that can create concrete work conditions for collaboration.

Collaboration as a significant item in the whole
structure of reward can also influence active behaviour.
In other words, a culture of positive reinforcement can
bring into existence positive sanctions and norms of
collaboration in an organisation system.   It is possible
to establish positive reinforcement as an ongoing culture
if the work groups are perceived as the forum through
which collaborative norms are to be fostered.   This is
not to deny a relevant role to individual autonomy.
Autonomy does not necessarily conflict with collective
norms and sanctions, provided that there is a common
attitude to the mission of the organisation.   The
development of suitable conceptions to explain the organisation and facilitate collaborative culture is a possibility for personnel functionaries to explore.   This is
where social sanction for the mission of an organisation
is relevant.   So far as the goals and purposes of an
organisation are clear to society, it can replace com-
petitiveness, the withholding of information and the dis-
tortion of inter-personal and intergroup communication in
the system.

(c)   The process consultation
      role

Process consultation, as distinguished from
"product" consultation, is a set of activities on the
part of a change agent that can help a client to perceive, understand and act upon process events occurring
in his environment.[30]

Process consultation involves skills that interpret
structural events in terms of process events, such as the
quality of communication, role perception by various
parties, patterns of influence, goal convergence versus
goal diffusion, the characteristics of the work group in
relation to decision-making, the quality of personal
growth as part of continuing learning culture and the
leadership role, which are essential in understanding the
operational dynamics of an organisation.   In fact, an
effective counselling role performed by the personnel
department can follow a process consultation approach,
which in essence would harmonise with an approach based
on new forms of work organisation.

(d)   The innovative role

The change agent role implies the ability to learn by
changing and to change while learning.   In this learning-
changing dynamics the personnel man as a change agent
is in a position to innovate in his own role through an
unfolding process that in another context can be expressed

as emergent work or an emerging role.[31]   This is a role
which can be determined neither by the self nor by
others, unless there is a constructive relation between
the self and others, within the context of the ongoing
relations of the personnel man.

It is suggested that to be effective in a non-
traditional organisational environment, a personnel man
will need to acquire these roles with all the implicit
and explicit values underlying them.

11.   The personnel man:
The challenge

We will now briefly outline some of the challenges,
dilemmas and frustrations that a personnel man is likely
to be confronted with in his proposed new role.   The
intention is not to discourage him in his mission, but
rather to present a realistic cognitive map.

The over-all perspective

Maccoby has made the significant point that the em-
phasis placed on a humanistic orientation in organisational dynamics may be an oversimplification of the
reality.[32]   There are employees in an organisation
possessing certain social characteristics that have
developed as an adaptation to the economic, social and
cultural conditions common to a specific group.   No
doubt many employees will respond to the new challenges
arising from a new form of work organisation with an apa-
thetic or negative attitude.   This may be due to their
belief that there is no genuine alternative to what they
have been accustomed to ever since childhood, a belief
in which they have the support of their social group.

It is not easy to dispel this belief, but it must
also be realised that there are employees who may not
respond to the opportunities offered by participative
design in a work system calling for additional psychic
energy and a commitment to certain ideals.   Different
employees will respond in different ways.   In this
situation a personnel man is expected to develop a sensitive understanding of these differences between one person
and another and, more significantly, between certain
social groups and others.   A personnel man will thus
have to balance the demands arising out of these varying
human characteristics in a complex organisation system so
that one model of organisation does not assert itself,
even if, from a humanistic point of view, it can be conceived as ideal.

The socio-economic and cultural power configuration
of a society is usually taken for granted by the management of an enterprise, which does not at all events consider them to be basic institutional factors whose effect
on people needs to be explored.   The values of profess-
ionalism that motivate a personnel man are usually confined to micro-changes and so organisational development
becomes an "encapsulated" approach.   The dynamics of
relations between an organisation and its social context
are often neglected.   Social sensitivity, in other
words, is something that will acquire more and more
importance for the personnel man because he will find
that there are far too many conflicting and contradictory
human forces at work from which it will be unrealistic to
run away.

One element in this over-all perspective will be the
view of an employee as a total person, an employee, a
member of his family and a member of the community, in
short a person with varied interests whose priorities are
not fixed.   In developing countries many public enterprises create an "island existence" for their employees -
the work system, housing facilities, an education system,
health care and facilities for the supply of consumer
goods and services.   In such a situation, to view an
employee in the limited role of a producer on the shop
floor or in an office will lead to an inadequate and un-
satisfactory strategy of development.   The composite
life that such an enclaved existence offers an employee
should figure in the personnel man's perspective.   The
personnel man will also find that this isolated existence
does not encompass the total person, who has an active
transactional relation with his outside environment.
He may have several inter-acting reference groups that
also influence his behaviour at work and at home.
Thorsrud's description of the local community scenario
is of great importance in this context.[33]

The point is that there cannot be one single form of
organisation system, just as there cannot be one universal type of employee wedded to certain basic values.
There are pluralities and multiplicities.   This does not
make the task of the management easy, but the real significance of the point is that the organisational design
problem is highly complex, a reality that a personnel man
will need to appreciate.

The systems approach

If he is to appreciate the diversity and contradic-
tions that the total-man concept signifies, the personnel
man will have to rise above his expertise and his limited
cognitive map and develop a systems orientation towards

148

men and organisations. Schon has ably argued that
organisations have reached a state beyond stability and
that in this state rapidity of change cannot be understood or dealt with by falling back on past experiences,
conventions and customs.[34]   The past provides only a
working hypothesis.   In other words, organisational
reality in the context of changeable and often unpredictable environmental forces encompasses stability and
change as co-existing forces.   This calls for a complex
balancing between changing structure and changing
behaviour, which becomes possible if an organisation
system is conceived in terms of multiplicity of inter-
acting variables and behaviour patterns, technologies at
work, communication, information and control mechanisms,
etc., are perceived so as to reflect the social reality
of an organisation rather than what one would like to see
as an ideal prototype.

The participative-research orientation

A participative, action research orientation in the
personnel man is likely to become increasingly relevant.
Action research, as Clark points out,[35] seeks to optimise
both scientific discoveries and the solution of practical
problems.   In a way, its objective is to operationalise
the dynamic relation between theory and practice.
Lewin's statement that a sound theory is a most practical
thing is at the root of action research.   Action research
reflects a concern both to solve practical problems in a
non-manipulative manner and to base reflection on the
action process, which can then become the core of scientific knowledge.   This scientific knowledge with its
solid basis can then lead to the next stage of action.

The dilemma brought about by the interplay of the
planning process and the implementation process is
familiar.   Although a tailor-made solution to this
dilemma cannot yet be devised, and probably never will
be, it is becoming more and more evident that an adaptive
planning process in which planning and implementation
form an integrated task can be instituted if the two sets
of persons cast in two different roles can collaborate
fruitfully.

The network of people

All this time we have been talking about the role of
the personnel man, which may give the impression that we
consider him to be the sole repository of innovative
action in an organisation.   This is not so.   The personnel man, in our _gestalt_, is seen as one who will need

to assume certain values, ideas, approaches and orientations consistent with the basic philosophy of new forms of human organisation but he is by no means seen as a lonely missionary.

It is appreciated that he is a member of a management team and that he also has inter-acting membership of various reference groups. His innovative role will therefore need to develop a network orientation. Herbst has described a network group as the converse of an autonomous group. "The members of a network are normally dispersed individually or in small sub-sets. It is only infrequently that they come together as a joint group in a work session and for direct communication. ... The basic characteristic of a network is the maintenance of long-term directive correlations, mutually facilitating achievement of a jointly recognised aim."[36] Our view is that the idea of the network as a potential work role will not necessarily remain confined to the personnel man. If a network system is to be effective, the idea will have to spread across the "leading parts" of an enterprise system. At the same time, the personnel man cannot ignore its working principle.

It is postulated that the network group in the management system will call for certain leadership skills, which have been described by Mintzberg.[37] We can mention these here:

(1) Peer skills - the ability to establish and maintain a network of contacts with equals.

(2) Leadership skills - the ability to deal with subordinates and the kinds of complication that are created by power, authority and dependence.

(3) Conflict-resolution skills - the ability to mediate conflict and to handle disturbances under psychological stress.

(4) Information-processing skills - the ability to build networks, extract and validate information and disseminate information effectively.

(5) Skills in decision-making in an unstructured setting - the ability to find problems and solutions when alternatives, information and objectives are ambiguous.

(6) Resource-allocation skills - the ability to decide among alternative uses of time and other scarce organisational resources.

(7) Entrepreneurial skills - the ability to take sensible risks and implement innovations.

(8) Skills of introspection - the ability to understand the position of a leader and his impact on the organisation.

Commenting on this list of desirable skills, Bennis observes that yet another critical leadership variable is the ability to define issues without aggravating the problems.[38] Perhaps this aspect, in addition to other compulsions, has led to the concept of the search conference as an extension of the strategy of participative design. The search conference, if one can articulate Merrelyn Emery's approach,[39] represents a way of understanding social realities with their complex issues and problems and seeks, in a learning atmosphere, to give effect, without recourse to conventional wisdom, to alternative approaches to the uncertainty that is often at the root of a problem.

The time horizon

Demands for new forms of work organisation, it is appreciated, have arisen out of a variety of social compulsions in developing and developed countries in pre-industrial, industrial and post-industrial societies. Whatever the characteristics of the social forces, the objective behind the search for a behavioural-structural solution to human systems design lies in a yearning for continuous improvements in the quality of human life as anchored in various human organisations.

In this perspective, a personnel man, without losing his grip on immediate issues and problems, must extend his time horizon beyond the immediate in order to embrace a comprehensive mosaic of the mission and its ideals. In a short-term perspective, certain segments of systemic issues will become important, whereas in intermediate and long-term perspectives, certain other issues will come into focus even in the present. In other words, the future has to be planned in the reality of the present, and past experience can at best provide a rough, hazy and incomplete indicator.

12. References

[1] Gyllenhammar, P.G.: People at work (London, Addison-Wesley Publishing Co., 1977).

[2] Litterer, J.A.: The analysis of organizations (New York, John Wiley, 1973).

3 Emery, F.E.: In pursuit of ideals (Canberra, Centre for Continuing Education, Australian National University, 1976).

4 Trist, Eric: "The concept of organizational ecology", in National Labour Institute Bulletin (New Delhi), December 1976.

5 McFarland, D.E.: Cooperation and conflict in personnel administration (New York, American Foundation for Management Research, 1962).

6 Herzberg, F.: Work and the nature of man (Cleveland, World Publishing Co., 1976).

7 Sokolik, S.L.: "Re-organise the personnel department?", in California Management Review, Vol. IX, No. 3, 1969.

8 Emery, F.E.: Futures we are in (Leiden, Martinus-Nijhoff, 1977).

9 Emery, F.E., et al.: Participative design (Canberra, Centre for Continuing Education, Australian National University, 1964).

10 Barker, R.: "Ecology and motivation", in Nebraska Symposium on Motivation (Lincoln, University of Nebraska Press, 1960).

11 Vroom, V.H.: Some personality determinants of the effects of participation (Englewood Cliffs, Prentice Hall, 1960).

12 Fromm, Erich: The sane society (London, Routledge and Kegan Paul, 1963).

13 Emery, F.E.: "Continuing education under a gum tree", in Australian Journal of Adult Education; "Another gum tree", unpublished paper (Canberra, Centre for Continuing Education, Australian National University, 1975 and 1976).

14 Kolb, D.A. (ed.), et al.: "preface", in Organizational Psychology (Englewood Cliffs, Prentice Hall, 1971).

15 Freire, Paulo: Cultural action for freedom (Harmondsworth, Penguin Books Ltd., 1972).

16 Schein, E.H.: "The individual, organization and the career: A conceptual scheme", D.A. Kolb in (ed.): Organizational Psychology (Englewood Cliffs, Prentice Hall, 1971).

[17] Super, D.E.: The psychology of careers (New York, Harper, 1957).

[18] Kubie, L.S.: "Some unresolved problems of the scientific career", in American Scientist, Vol. 41 and Vol. 42, 1953 and 1954.

[19] O'Toole, J. (ed.): Work and the quality of life (Cambridge, Mass., MIT Press, 1974).

[20] Roeber, J.: Social change at work (London, Duckworth, 1975).

[21] Odaka, K.: Toward industrial democracy (Cambridge, Mass., Harvard University Press, 1975).

[22] Maccoby, M.: "Changing work: the Bolivar Project", in Working Papers for a New Society, Summer 1975.

[23] Walton, R.E., et al.: A behavioural theory of labour negotiations (New York, McGraw-Hill, 1965).

[24] De, Nitish, R.: "An action plan for effective industrial relations in the public sector", in Indian Journal of Industrial Relations, (New Delhi), Vol. 8, No. 3, 1973.

[25] Qvale, T.U.: "A Norwegian strategy for democratization of industry", in Human Relations (London), Vol. 29, No. 5, 1976.

[26] Argyris, C., et al.: Theory in practice: Increasing professional effectiveness (San Francisco, Jossey-Bass, 1974).

[27] Mulder, M.: The daily power game (Leiden, Martinus-Nijhoff, 1977).

[28] Harrison, R.: "Understanding your organization's character", in Harvard Business Review (Cambridge, Mass.), May/June 1972.

[29] De, Nitish, R.: "Erikson's testament of hope: A dimension to quality of work life", in National Labour Institute Bulletin (New Delhi), August 1977.

[30] Schein, E.H.: Process consultation: Its role in organization development (Reading, Addison-Wesley, 1969).

[31] Cummings, T.G., et al.: Management of work (Kent, Kent State University Press, 1977).

[32] Maccoby, M.: The gamesman (New York, Simon and Schuster, 1976).

[33] Thorsrud, Einar: Democracy at work and perspectives on the quality of working life in Scandinavia (Geneva, International Institute for Labour Studies, 1976).

[34] Schon, D.A.: Beyond the stable state (New York, Random House, 1971).

[35] Clark, A.W.: "Introduction", in A.W. Clark (ed.): Experimenting with Organizational Life (New York, Plenum Press, 1976).

[36] Herbst, P.G.: Alternatives to hierarchies (Leiden, Martinus-Nijhoff, 1976).

[37] Mintzberg, H.: The nature of managerial work, (New York, Harper and Row, 1973).

[38] Bennis, W.G.: The unconscious conspiracy (New York, AMACOM, 1976).

[39] Emery, M.: Searching (Canberra, Centre for Continuing Education, Australian National University, 1976).

WORK ORGANISATION AND REMUNERATION – NEW TRENDS IN WAGES AND INCENTIVES

5

Håkan Lundgren and Jan-Peder Norstedt*

1. Introduction

Wage systems follow no standard pattern. They vary
from one workplace to another. The nature of the production operation and the technology used, as well as the
nature of the organisation itself, determine how the work
will actually be performed, and this in turn affects the
allocation of wages between different jobs and different
individuals. Thus, the problems encountered in wage
determination in small batch manufacturing will not be
the same as those met with in automated processes, nor
will the same criteria apply in a production department,
for example, and in a maintenance department. However,
despite these variations, it is possible to distinguish
some main trends:

- There appears to be a growing tendency towards a
  fixed-wage component. The traditional piece-work
  wage system is being replaced either by a premium
  wage which includes a relatively large component of
  fixed wages or by fixed wages combined with some
  form of payment by results. In some cases a pure
  fixed-wage system has been introduced.

- In the new wage systems production premiums and payment by results are often calculated and paid for
  the production group or a production department as
  a whole. A common argument in favour of the group
  premium is that it stimulates co-operation and a
  common effort to improve results; it also means
  that any yardsticks applied can embrace the result
  of the operation as a whole.

---

* Håkan Lundgren and Jan-Peder Norstedt are
Directors at the Swedish Employers' Confederation.

- Many of the new wage systems call for a new approach to the way wages are adjusted to job requirements. Most people would agree that the more demanding jobs merit a higher remuneration than the simpler ones. At the same time, the need to safeguard income security has often upset wage differentials based on job evaluation when transfers were considered. Attempts have been made to solve these problems in a way that allows for flexibility in the organisation together with a guarantee of individual income security, in addition to an economic reward commensurate with job requirements.

- Examples of the forms of individual competency often taken into consideration in determining new wage systems are professional experience, skill in performing a variety of jobs, length of employment in the enterprise, familiarity with the work processes and an understanding of the technological and economic aspects.

- Some new wage systems are reviewed on a monthly basis.

- Many people now feel a keen interest in wage systems that can be applied both to the manual workers and to the supervisors and other salaried employees in production units, particularly where these groups of employees work together. So far, however, such schemes are rare.

2. The adaptation of remuneration systems to changes in work organisation

With the introduction of new forms of work organisation, production has often been broken down into more autonomous groups. Individual roles have changed in content and have acquired additional and more interesting functions. These changes in production often necessitate a change in the existing wages system, for example:

(a) Many enterprises have abandoned the functional organisation of production. Instead, machines are grouped on a production flow basis and workers are organised into groups or teams, along the production line. In group organisation, individuals work together to achieve a common goal. Under such a system individual payments on a piece-rate basis are not feasible, since this would run counter to the concept of group co-operation. A bonus based on the performance of the group, on the other hand, acts as an incentive to boost production.

(b) In a production group, the workers not only carry out the various tasks allotted to them but are also responsible for the co-ordination of these tasks. Group organisation calls for flexibility so that each person can give his services wherever they are most needed; in other words, there is job rotation at the worker's own initiative. This requires new methods of job evaluation and new guidelines for wage differentials. These differentials must be based on the over-all work role of the individual and not on the specific task which he happens to be performing at a given moment.

Of course, wage differentials are required even in group organisation. Job roles and competency levels rarely match. Even in an autonomous production group, newcomers must be gradually trained and their skills improved so that they can take on more difficult assignments. Levelling the wage differentials between the experienced and the inexperienced, the skilled and the unskilled provides no incentive for personal development. Wage differentials must therefore be introduced in such a way that they encourage career development without hampering organisational flexibility.

3.   Basic features of a new
     wages system

Experience has shown that a revision of wages and incentives is often essential when new forms of work organisation are introduced. Several factors have to be borne in mind in this respect. Safeguarding the level of present earnings is an important consideration. People are very alarmed by the possibility of a cut in their wages. This means that both job evaluation and incentive schemes and payment-by-result systems must be designed accordingly. Furthermore, the wages system must account for individual variations in terms of experience, professional skill or demanding job requirements. In addition, new forms of work organisation should aim to interest workers in their production output; they should feel that they stand to benefit from the improvements that result. Changes in work organisation can occur frequently, however, and so output and payment by results must be measured often enough to take changes in the work system and in individual roles into consideration. Finally, it is highly desirable to harmonise the wage systems of both white and blue-collar workers by applying similar evaluation systems as far as possible.

Each of these factors will now be examined separately.

3.1 A fresh look at job evaluation

There are three important trends in connection with job evaluation:

(1) Job evaluation and wage differentials according to job requirements are based more and more on the over-all work role of the individual and not on the particular task which he is performing at a given moment, nor on his rotation between different tasks and different parts in a production system. There are two reasons for this. First, it allows for flexibility in work organisation, since flexibility is hampered if job rotation leads to changes in wages. Second, it also provides for income security. Some enterprises have signed labour agreements guaranteeing income security in the event of transfer. These contractual provisions ensure that the individual will retain his former wages for a certain period if he is transferred to a lower paid job.

(2) Simpler job evaluation systems are being introduced. The so-called "point system" is still the most common type of job evaluation system for production work; however, many enterprises have begun to use simple classification systems instead. Simpler, less laborious job evaluation methods are naturally of great interest to small and medium-sized enterprises. Many large enterprises are interested in simpler systems as well. In fact, in most cases job grading is the same whether one uses a simple or a more complex system. These simpler classification systems are similar in structure to those used for white-collar jobs. They therefore represent a step towards a common job evaluation system for manual and white-collar workers.

(3) There are many examples of compensation for physically demanding jobs and unpleasant working conditions through separate wage supplements awarded outside the job evaluation framework. There are many reasons for this. By dividing the concept of "difficulty" into its two main parts (job requirements and unpleasant working conditions) it is easier to understand the reasons for differentiating wages on the basis of these two factors. The aim of differentiation based on competency requirements is to encourage and create interest in personal development, in the acquisition of greater responsibility and in advancement to more demanding duties. Differentiation on the basis of physical difficulty and unpleasant working conditions aims at compensating for such working conditions. It therefore becomes easier to see more

158

clearly this difference and negotiate on compensation for unpleasant working conditions.

A prerequisite for job evaluation is a classification system consisting of one or more scales, in which each grade or class is defined in terms of the relevant job requirements. Every job is then placed in the relevant class.

The "position classification system - salaried employees" is an example of this kind of system. The division of each job family into different job levels provides a rough classification scale for job evaluation. This classification system is used in Sweden for practically all salaried work in industry and commerce and in some other fields as well.

The position classification system was originally designed mainly for use in preparing salary statistics, but it also provides guidelines for determining the remuneration of salaried employees in individual enterprises.

Classification models of this kind have also been designed for some industries as a whole, such as the petroleum industry and the motor vehicle service and repair industry.

The tables on the next page illustrate some classification scales designed for the motor vehicle service and repair industry. They are included in an appendix to the motor vehicle and tractor agreement between the Swedish Motor Trade Employers' Association and the Swedish Metal Workers' Union. This appendix gives classification scales for vehicle repairs, service and checking, electrical repairs, preparation for delivery, bodywork, paintwork and spare-parts handling. The scales are intended to serve as examples which can be adjusted and applied locally in different enterprises.

Thus, in these cases; simple classification scales have been constructed for job evaluation purposes in different occupational fields, and can be illustrated by the simple model in figure 2. Like factor evaluation or point-rating schemes, job classification schemes are models intended to reflect the respective position of jobs, but to some extent the two types of scheme reflect this position from different angles.

The point-rating system concentrates on the analysis of the content and requirements of the job. The classification system emphasises the over-all nature of the job and reflects possible channels for development and promotion. A major impetus behind the development of schemes

Figure 1   Examples of position groupings: vehicle repairs

Position	Position description
Motor technicians	Carry out independent work that makes especially high demands on technical and practical knowledge. Locate the more serious faults and are familiar with all jobs in the repair shop. Carry out independently any repair and maintenance jobs that arise, including locating faults in all areas, even fairly simple operations involving welding and realigning (bodywork). Can, when necessary, instruct and supervise, and even deputise for the foreman or other supervisors in the shop.
1st mechanics	Undertake independently most of the repair and maintenance jobs that arise, including location of faults in all areas, even bodywork which does not require realigning (replacing body components) and the more simple welding jobs. When necessary, can instruct and supervise.
2nd mechanics	Undertake independently most of the repair and maintenance jobs that arise, including location of faults in all areas, except the more extensive and complicated jobs on gear-boxes, differentials, injection pumps and so on. Alternatively, undertake all repairs including location of faults in at least one major area such as engine or transmission. Undertake the more simple bodywork which does not require welding and realigning.
3rd mechanics	Undertake independently the more simple repair and maintenance jobs, and some more complicated jobs under supervision. Alternatively undertake independently all jobs on at least one type of equipment (e.g. brakes).
Assistant mechanics	Undertake, under supervision, the more simple repair and maintenance jobs. Alternatively undertake independently the more simple jobs within a limited area.

Service and checking

Position	Position description
Express-service mechanics	Undertake independently all repair jobs requiring little time. Responsible for a limited spare-part stock, attend to customers and see to the records for invoicing.
Service mechanics	Undertake independently all service, checking and maintenance jobs that arise, together with the necessary adjustments, and relatively simple repair jobs.
Serviceman	Undertakes independently service and checking jobs and makes the necessary adjustments. Alternatively undertakes independently greasing, changing oil, washing (bodywork and engine), polishing and undersealing.

Figure 2   Classification scales for job evaluation

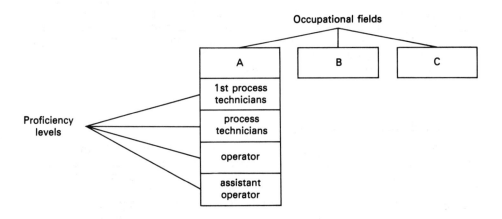

like this has been the desire to find a simpler system of job evaluation.

Many enterprises which have not previously intro- duced job evaluation systems now feel a need to system- atise their evaluation of different jobs.   At the same time they feel that factor evaluation and point rating are too laborious, although they provide a more specific and accurate description of the various conditions that have to be considered in the valuation.   However, as mentioned earlier, they make job rotation or interchange- ability more difficult.

3.2   Wage differentials and
      individual proficiency
      and competence

Job evaluation is just one component in wage deter- mination.   The skill and competence of the individual is another component to be considered.   Merit rating is usually used as an aid in determining individual wage increments.

In some wage systems, an alternative to traditional merit rating has been applied.   Agreements between management and unions were reached regarding special personal wage increments based on simple, quantifiable individual factors.   Examples of such individual factors are versatility (measured as the number of jobs which the individual can execute), experience (measured as number of years in the trade, or in the company), education use- ful on the job, etc.   These factors are not considered together.   Instead, personal wage increments are deter- mined for each factor separately.

161

The most important reason why this method is used is
that it takes account of the competency of the individual
clearly and consistently.   It has often proved easier
for employers and employees to reach agreement over this
type of personal wage increment than over individual wage
differences based on merit rating, which can sometimes
lead to subjective judgements.

3.3   Output and wages, payment by results

The whole issue of relating wages to output and to
efficiency continues to be debated in many countries and
enterprises.   The so-called payment-by-results system
has been criticised on several counts - because, for
example, it does not guarantee income security, it is
hard to apply to white-collar workers, it introduces different treatment for white and blue-collar workers, and
so on.   Those opposed to this form of wage scheme have
advocated a return to a fixed-wage system, irrespective
of the level of output achieved.   At this juncture, it
should be emphasised that payment by results really
encompasses two distinct systems: namely, pure piece-
rate schemes, and premium or bonus payment schemes for
output over and above a predetermined standard.

Recent studies in Sweden, where new forms of work
organisation are becoming more and more common, have
shown that over the past 15 years the proportion of pure
piece-rate schemes in enterprises has declined from
46 per cent to 14 per cent.   Similarly, the proportion
of premium or bonus systems has increased from 24 per
cent to 39 per cent.   Fixed-wage systems, on the other
hand, also increased from 30 per cent to 47 per cent.

During the same period, the proportion of group wage
systems increased from 38 per cent to 58 per cent and the
proportion of individual bonuses declined from 62 per
cent to 42 per cent.

More recently, however, straight fixed-wage systems
appear to be losing ground to payment-by-results systems.
This is particularly noticeable in small enterprises
where during the past three years the percentage of
payment-by-results systems has increased by almost 25 per
cent.

How do these different wage systems affect efficiency?   Two important findings will be discussed here:

(1) It is possible to develop new payment-by-
results schemes which both satisfy the need for income
security and at the same time increase efficiency.   We

have many examples of successful wage reforms where a traditional piece-rate system has been replaced by a fixed-wage scheme with differentials for competency and combined with bonus incentives - some enterprises adopting this approach have achieved productivity improvements of 20 to 25 per cent. At the same time, such reforms have greatly increased income security for the employees.

There are two ways of combining income security with payment by results. The first way is to design the relationship between production results and wages in such a manner that fluctuations in earnings are small. This entails a fixed-wage portion and a variable bonus portion. The size of the bonus is determined according to acceptable variations in earnings.

This method of providing income security also has its weaknesses. Since the degree of income security is determined by the nature of the relationship between production results and wages, upward income variations are limited to the same degree as downward variations. The result is that by guaranteeing the income security of employees, their possibility of increasing their incomes by improving their results may be restricted. This causes problems. If better results lead to insignificant increases in income, there is a risk that the employees will come to the conclusion that the incentives are meaningless.

The second way is to combine payment by results with a guaranteed wage level. With this method the question of income security becomes independent of the design of the incentive portion of the wages.

With this solution we can combine 100 per cent income security with substantial bonuses for improvements in productivity. This is accomplished as follows. A fixed-wage level is set in accordance with the current productivity level. Bonuses are paid only if productivity is higher than this level. Income security can be maintained by raising the fixed wage once a year in accordance with the average improvement in results obtained during the year. The new fixed wage then applies for the new productivity level, and bonuses can once again be paid when productivity rises above this new level. We normally call this system Production Profit Sharing.

There are two main justifications for this solution:

- it eliminates the conflict between income security and payment by results;

- it encourages and rewards a long-range positive productivity trend. One might also say that this wage system retains reward but abolishes punishment.

(2) A changeover to a straight fixed-wage system without any incentive component based on productivity has, in most cases, led to considerable losses in efficiency, at least in some Swedish enterprises.

These two findings are supported by the Swedish Employers' Confederation's study The condemned piecework. The results of this study may be summarised as follows:

- when a changeover was made from a piece-work to a fixed-wage system, efficiency losses of, on average, 15 to 25 per cent were reported;

- when a changeover was made from a conventional piece-work to a premium system, efficiency gains of, on average, 5 to 10 per cent were reported;

- when a changeover was made from a fixed-wage to a bonus incentive wages system, efficiency gains of, on average, 25 to 35 per cent were reported;

- in most cases, no significant changes were reported regarding quality, absenteeism and personnel turnover.

What, then, are the reasons for efficiency losses when a company changes over to a straight fixed-wage system? It is not that the working pace declines. In most cases, workers carry on at about the same pace as before. The most important reasons are of a more indirect nature. Workers seem to lose interest in taking any initiative. They appear to be no longer so interested in spontaneously solving problems on their own. The level of utilisation of both production equipment and working time declines. When production equipment is used less, capital costs rise. Increased capital cost is one factor which has often been overlooked in the debate surrounding payment by results.

Increases in productivity do not result simply from steady increases in the working pace - by workers running instead of walking. Rather, they are dependent on a continuous process of day-to-day rationalisation, on a will and a capacity to use the production equipment in a sensible and effective manner. The design of the wages system can play an important role in this respect.

Payment by results also seems to play a major role in supporting the work organisation and production administration. Incentive components generate the employees'

interest in following production results and in discussing trends. Experience shows that discussions of such
a nature often cease when payment by results is abolished.

So far we have dealt with the issues relating to the
bonus or premium which is a component of a fixed or other
form of wage system. As indicated earlier, this premium
is payable only if productivity rises above a certain
predetermined standard. To determine this standard we
have to be able to measure productivity at the group or
department level.

Well developed work-measurement methods exist for
measuring the efficiency of single operations. Other
methods also exist for measuring the economic results of
the enterprise as a whole, or for major divisions of the
enterprise, by using financial ratios. There is a gap,
however, between work measurement and the use of financial indicators to assess the financial gains to be
devoted to bonuses. Some attempts have been made to
fill in this gap. The processing time of the product,
the value added by processing and the material yield
(i.e. the ratio between the quantity of finished products
and the quantity of the original material) are examples
of such attempts. Nevertheless, a great deal remains to
be done in this area. We regard output measurement for
small groups and for departments, with a view to establishing equitable standards of performance, as a field
where development work is urgently needed.

3.4 Wages for manual and for
     white-collar workers

Throughout the development of wages systems efforts
have been made to harmonise the conditions of manual
workers and white-collar workers. To some extent, the
existing differences are due to historical reasons, but
it should also be remembered that in some cases the wages
policies of the two groups' unions have had different
goals.

In direct production activities, the common practice
has been to adopt some form of payment by results. For
salaried employees fixed monthly remuneration, differ-
entiated according to individual competence, continues to
be widespread. Payment by results has also been used in
certain service groups; we have the example of commis-
sions paid to sales staff, premium-wage schemes for some
office jobs and various systems of managerial bonuses.

Nevertheless, it would still be true to say that
manual work and white-collar work are generally paid
according to different systems. So long as the main

form of payment by results was the classical piece-work
wage system, there was a plausible explanation for this
division.   A payment-by-results system that is based on
the efficiency of the individual operations can be
applied only to jobs in which that kind of efficiency can
be measured.   It is very difficult to measure the efficiency of the individual operations that constitute most
white-collar jobs;   hence the customary use of fixed
wages.   On the production side, too, there are many jobs
where efficient performance cannot be measured either,
with the result that some production units have been paid
under a mixture of the payment-by-results and the hourly
wage systems.   Sometimes it may even be necessary for a
worker to change from one kind of wage system to another
when he moves from one task to another.

None the less, just because it is difficult to
measure the efficiency of the individual operations that
constitute a job, this does not mean that the workers
doing these jobs cannot influence the efficiency of the
activity as a whole.   On the contrary, they can do a
great deal to influence the way results develop.

We have seen that payment-by-result systems are
becoming increasingly linked to group wage schemes in
which the premium component is based on the joint production result of a group or department.   Payment-by-result
systems based not only on the efficiency of individual
operations but also on other factors that are essential
to the end result are being developed.   When a payment-
by-results system is based on the effort of a particular
production unit (group, department or even sometimes a
whole enterprise), it becomes difficult to account for
differences in wage systems between the various categories of personnel.   After all, the results now reflect
the combined effort of all the members of the group or
unit.   Why, then, should they not be all included in the
same wage system and enjoy the fruits, if any, of their
common work?   Why should different categories of
employees in a production unit, whose joint effort provides the basis for the premium wage component, be paid
according to different wage systems?   Recent trends
suggest that, when new forms of work organisation are
applied, these differences gradually diminish.   The
emergence of a fixed-wage component for production work
is a move in that direction.   We have also seen several
examples of wage systems that cover not only the production workers in a production unit but also the supervisors and other white-collar workers.   Changes in the
position or points system and in methods of job evaluation are also helping to bring about a more uniform wage
system which applies to the various categories of
employees and aligns them more closely with each other.

Thus the demarcation line between the wage systems used for manual workers and those used for white-collar workers is becoming less distinct. This does not mean, however, that in the end one kind of wages will be applied to everybody. The design of any wage system will continue to be adapted to the conditions and values prevailing in the unit or enterprise where the system is to be used. What it does mean, however, is that dividing lines based on employees' organisational affiliations will gradually disappear.

4. Design of a wages system: Some concluding remarks

In this chapter we have discussed various problems and trends encountered in setting up wage systems. Our aim has not been to suggest a perfect system, but to point out the implications that new forms of work organisation can have on wages. What characterises a "good" wages system, in our opinion, is that:

(a) it is adapted to the nature of the operation, be it group work or individual work;

(b) employees are able to reap the rewards when they have achieved better results and to enjoy a differentiation in income that is based on varying degrees of competency;

(c) it satisfies the demand for income security with the need for incentives based on higher or better output;

(d) more demanding jobs, or those that are strenuous, are compensated for;

(e) wages systems for blue and white-collar workers are moving closer together whenever possible; and if both categories of personnel are employed in the same working group, the same principles for determining wage would be applied to each.

With the introduction of new forms of work organisation, we indicated that a new approach to job evaluation has developed, that there is a trend towards combining a fixed portion of wages with another component to allow for job requirements, for individual competency and for a premium to be paid for output over and above an expected standard. This premium tends to be a group rather than an individual premium.

Naturally, these mechanisms for establishing wages continue to be conducted within the framework of the existing negotiating machinery. However, with group work, it has become easier for joint project groups to discuss such issues as systems of job evaluation, the measurement of a group's output, wage differentials for competence, and so on, and to propose solutions to the negotiating partners.   Thus in many enterprises a new and a more open way has been devised for dealing with wages.   Both management and workers have gained an insight into the different aspects of wage determination, and the result has been a greater spirit of co-operation between them.

INTRODUCING AND DEVELOPING
NEW FORMS OF WORK ORGANISATION

6

George Kanawaty*

In recent years, many enterprises in various parts of the world have chosen to rearrange their activities in accordance with new forms of work organisation. In some, these were introduced as an experimental phase involving a certain job, a specific work station or a particular department. In others, such as the Volvo plant at Kalmar[1] in Sweden, and some merchant shipping companies in Norway,[2] they have become a permanent feature in the design of the total operational activity.

Recent work indicates that this approach is equally as applicable to developing countries as it is to more advanced countries, although social and cultural differences dictate locally developed solutions. The level of education of the workers involved in work reorganisation does not appear to be a determining factor in their failure or success. Thus good results were obtained by shop-floor, almost illiterate workers in some enterprises in developing countries as well as by highly qualified engineers and professional staff.[3]

The methods adopted in introducing the desired change have varied from one case to another, depending on the objective to be achieved, the particular problems and situation facing the enterprise and the scope of the modification to be introduced in the organisation. True, there is no such thing as a universal strategy of change, to be followed by each enterprise, in any given situation. Nevertheless, there are certain underlying notions that can assist a manager in steering a safer

---

* George Kanawaty is Chief of the Management Development Branch at the International Labour Office (ILO) in Geneva.

course towards a workable change in his organisation. This chapter proposes to discuss them. At the outset, it indicates factors that can trigger a need for change in organisations. It then provides a guide to the development of new forms of work organisation and points out the pitfalls that can be avoided in introducing the change. Finally, three short case studies show how the new work organisation was introduced in three different situations; a production plant in Sweden, a post office in India, and a forwarding and handling enterprise in Tanzania.

1. A point of departure: Redesigning work - when and why?

New forms of work organisation have been introduced in many enterprises simply because management has been faced with certain problems of an operational or behavioural and social nature and a better work design was though to contribute to greater efficiency and higher job satisfaction. In other cases, however, management has taken the initiative in introducing change in anticipation of problems to come, or from the conviction that work can be rendered more productive and yet more satisfying. In other cases still, the employees or their representatives have come forward with ideas for modifying the organisation of work with a view to achieving basically the same objectives.

Three major reasons, either individually or in combination, normally contribute to sparking an interest in job redesign:

- Operational reasons

- Personnel and behavioural reasons

- Social reasons.

Operational reasons

Many working methods exist either as a matter of convenience or by tradition. In several cases, the introduction of new technology, of new products or of new operational objectives has been made without due consideration for their effect on job holders, or on the operational process itself.[4] As an example, the introduction of an extra multipurpose machine in a plant to cope with an upsurge of demand for a certain product may influence the balance of operations for other products. The fragmentation of jobs with the ostensible purpose of augmenting specialisation and increasing productivity can

introduce boredom into the job or deprive a person of his
initiative so far as to result in shoddy workmanship or
indifference to work.   In some instances, the fluctuat-
ing patterns of demand, for example seasonal changes or
a continuously changing product line, create the need for
more flexibility in organisations.

In many cases, therefore, a host of operational
reasons such as the desire for higher productivity,
better streamlining of operations or new technology, the
urge to reduce waste or lower costs or the search for
better quality and service, motivate a manager to want
to reorganise his work.

Personnel and behavioural reasons

When new forms of work organisation were introduced
in the early sixties in Norway and Sweden, reasons of a
personnel and behavioural nature were more compelling
than operational reasons.   True, there were operational
reasons as well, but managers were more preoccupied with
serious problems of high turnover, absenteeism and complaints and grievances.   There were also difficulties
in recruitment for a great number of jobs that opera-
tionally were considered effective but did not appeal to
workers because they were too monotonous, resulted in
high strain, offered no challenge or creativity or
reduced a worker's chances of communicating or inter-
acting with colleagues.   These problems were by no means
restricted to Scandinavia.   In many countries, alienation from work, low morale and several other symptoms of
malaise at work have given concern to managers and preci-
pitated the desire for a change in work methods and
practices and in the working environment.

Social reasons

As mentioned earlier, many managers have taken the
initiative in redesigning work from conviction or in
anticipation of problems that might arise from a changing
environment.   It is a fact that educational standards
are mounting and that the gradual rise in the standard of
living is accompanied by a rise in the level of aspira-
tions and expectations.   It is also a fact that in many
parts of the world family ties are becoming looser and
permissiveness and liberalism are gaining ground both at
home and throughout the educational phase of life.   It
is therefore only natural to expect some erosion of the
formal autocratic authority at work.[5]   In many parts of
the world experience shows that people do not always do
what they are told by those in authority at work or

171

accept that their supervisors always know better, nor is
it possible to secure unquestioned loyalty through
economic rewards alone.[6]

Furthermore, as society itself becomes engulfed in
more calls for democracy and for participation as a
natural process of political decision making, it is hard
to see how we can draw a dividing line between the
private man and the working man or between the social
environment and the working environment.

It is in response to these external winds of change
and not necessarily because of immediate internal problems that new forms of work organisation are being introduced in many enterprises today.

Considering the options

Many attempts at redesigning work have been doomed
to failure owing to the inability of management to make
a clear and objectively <u>a priori</u> assessment of the
chances of success or failure. So-called "experiments
in new forms of work organisation" are launched without
adequate reflection on whether conditions are really
favourable for their introduction.

In essence, a manager should first reflect carefully
on whether conditions are really favourable and, if not,
whether he should attempt to influence them or postpone
or abandon the reorganisation.

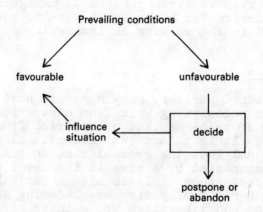

Several scholars such as Bekhard[7] and Greiner[8] set
certain conditions whose presence would be favourable to
introducing change in organisations. Among the various
factors cited, the following are perhaps among the more
important:

172

(i) There is an evident pressure for change and the diagnosis of specific problems is more or less clear.

(ii) There is leadership in the form of a key line executive, a key staff specialist or an outside consultant to steer the change through.

(iii) A favourable working climate, collaboration between line and staff people and good prospects of the inclusion of the key people are all present.

(iv) Tangible results can be expected.

(v) The system rewards people for the effort of changing as well as for the end results.

(vi) The attitude of the staff representatives to the change is positive.

Needless to say, such favourable conditions do not always prevail. The issue is then whether to influence the situation, to postpone the effort or to abandon it from the start. In reaching the decision, it may be useful to take such steps as:

(i) Assessing objectively whether the change is necessary and where; which department, which job and who will be affected. Try to anticipate the resistance that is likely to be generated as a result of conflicting interests of various groups. Are you able to commit yourself fully to the change process and to devote the necessary time and energy to seeing it through.

(ii) Having a preliminary talk with some people in the organisation who may be involved. This would include key people in line and staff and the unions. The purpose is to see how much support and interest in job design there is on the one hand, and on the other to listen to all possible demands or warnings concerning the side effects of the experiment. For example, this preliminary talk may indicate that the unions expect a revision of the wages and incentive systems as a result or that additional resources will need to be allocated for training purposes and so on.

(iii) Arranging for a seminar or a talk by an outsider or a specialist on new forms of work

organisation.   Allow enough inter-action and
discussion with the key people involved.

(iv)   Arranging for a visit by the key people
       involved to a site where new forms of work
       organisation have been introduced.

(v)   Getting the people involved to see the problems
       inherent in the present design (operational
       and/or behavioural/social) and inviting sugges-
       tions for improvement.   Consider whether these
       suggestions can be harnessed to a more positive
       and participative effort towards work reorgani-
       sation.

(vi)   Assessing the usefulness of a change agent in
       your particular situation, and whether his
       presence is likely to influence the sequence of
       change events positively.   Have you a suitable
       change agent in your organisation or do you
       need to consider an outside alternative?

These proposed courses of action could be taken
individually or in combination.   Thus, a study tour or
a visit may be followed by a seminar, or a preliminary
talk with key personnel may prove that the conditions are
favourable for a change, so that the actual planning can
start almost immediately.

So far, there has been no declared will that a
reorganisation of work shall really take place.   It is
simply an exercise in assessing whether conditions are
favourable, and to what extent they can be made so.
At the same time this exercise uncovers the possible
difficulties ahead.   This is crucial in deciding whether
to proceed with the change or to postpone it. All along,
this decision has to be made with respect to a realistic
level of expectations.   This will avoid a great deal of
possible frustration among those who expect the reorganisation to be a cure for all ills.

In certain situations, the decision to postpone or
abandon the work is almost obvious.   This is particularly
the case when there is a strong industrial relations
conflict, or when the unions do not sufficiently support
the endeavour, feeling that other issues merit a higher
priority, or when it is obvious that it will be difficult
to devote the necessary time and energy to the process.

2.   The approach to work reorganisation

Before going into any detail, it is useful to bear
in mind two important notions concerning the approach to

be followed.   First, the very core of this process of
change is participation by the people involved themselves
in redesigning their work.   In contrast, therefore, with
traditional consultancy, where a consultant makes the
diagnosis and prescribes solutions, or with process consultation, where the consultant "helps the client to perceive, understand and act upon process events which occur
in the client's environment",[9] in contrast, then, with
these approaches, the centre of gravity here, whether it
is in the diagnosis or in the development of a modified
organisation, lies in the working group.   Change also
proceeds at the pace at which the group is able to perceive it, introduce it and apply it.   A change agent
plays a catalytic role more than anything else.   There
are, of course, certain steps that need to be taken to
facilitate the work of the group or groups created for
this purpose but, by and large, they can be regarded as
subsiding.

     The second important notion is that the traditional
approaches to organisational change and improving effectiveness tend to examine a working situation either from
an operational point of view or from a social point of
view.   Thus, in many cases, specialists in inventory
control are asked to examine inventory control problems
and specialists in maintenance management or in salesman-
ship are brought in to revise the operational methods of
maintenance or of sales.   If behavioural problems do
manifest themselves, then behavioural scientists and
solutions in this field are sought.   In the approach
proposed for introducing new forms of work organisation,
both the technical and the social systems are considered
together for a given working situation, and the change
proposed is examined with respect to its effect on the
socio-technical system of the particular job.   The proposed solution is an optimum one aiming at maximising the
operational and behavioural outcome.   As a result of the
two above considerations, careful and patient preparation
and implementation are essential for success.   While
there is no such thing as a universal approach to be
followed in each case, the observances of certain rules
and guidelines can increase the chances of success.

     In his work at Shell UK, Hill identified nine
steps.[10]   These consisted in: initial scanning of the
production system, its characteristics and problems;
identification of unit operations and their role in the
production process;   identification of key process variances from standards and their inter-relations;   analysis
of the social system;   analysis of men's perception of
their roles;   analysis of maintenance activities and
variances;   analysis of supply and user systems and their
effect on production;   identification of environmental
forces affecting the operations of a refinery;

and, finally, making proposals for change. As can be
seen, some of these steps focus on the operational or
technical system and others on the social system. Some
other guidelines have been produced by other writers.
Hackman, for example, proposes guidelines for avoiding
pitfalls.[11] Others suggest certain approaches with
varying degrees of detail.[12] To a large extent, however,
most of the guidelines mentioned by various writers and
practitioners have been put forward with respect to a
particular enterprise or work situation, for example the
case of Shell UK mentioned above. This is understandable,
since it is difficult to duplicate conditions from one
situation to another. Because of this, the six-steps
approach suggested below (see figure 1) should be looked
at in a pragmatic way and adjusted, whenever necessary,
to suit the particular job situation.

Step 1: Identifying and diagnosing
the work system

In this initial step, one needs to select and de-
limit the job to be studied. The selection may be based
on operational or behavioural/personnel reasons (for
example low productivity, high degree of waste or lack of
interest and involvement in the job, higher absenteeism
and turnover). However, managers may also wish to
introduce new forms of work organisation for social
reasons such as those mentioned earlier. If this is the
case, one has to choose between the random selection of
a job to be reorganised and a more purposive selection
where the chances of success may be greater. This is
equally true of new forms of work organisation when
introduced in an enterprise for the first time. In such
cases, among the jobs to be selected are some that offer
little challenge and variety and where the supervisor and
the work team are receptive to new ideas. An added
advantage would be a task that is repeated elsewhere in
the plant. This could allow the use of a control group,
on the one hand, and a quicker diffusion of results if
the organisation proves to be successful, on the other.
Further clues to selecting jobs are those where there is
an overcomplicated work flow, a duplication of effort or
an unclear responsibility.[13]

Delimiting a job means deciding on the starting
point for the job under study and on the end point. By
implication this leads to a definition of the people
involved in performing that job whether directly or in a
staff or service capacity.

In this first step, a diagnosis of the socio-
technical system is then carried out. This means taking
stock of:

176

Figure 1   Guidelines for developing new forms of work organisation

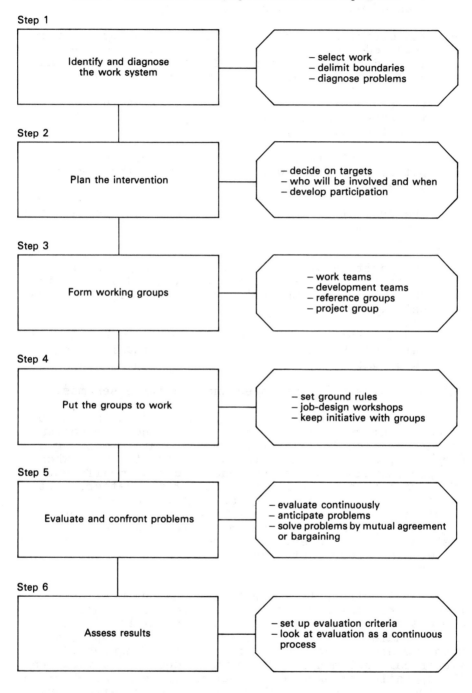

Step 1

| Identify and diagnose the work system | — select work
— delimit boundaries
— diagnose problems |

Step 2

| Plan the intervention | — decide on targets
— who will be involved and when
— develop participation |

Step 3

| Form working groups | — work teams
— development teams
— reference groups
— project group |

Step 4

| Put the groups to work | — set ground rules
— job-design workshops
— keep initiative with groups |

Step 5

| Evaluate and confront problems | — evaluate continuously
— anticipate problems
— solve problems by mutual agreement or bargaining |

Step 6

| Assess results | — set up evaluation criteria
— look at evaluation as a continuous process |

(a)   the range of activities performed, with an indication of whom they are performed by;

(b)   the output and input of work, the quality standards required and the range of variations from the desired targets in terms of quality, quantity and cost, and the reasons for these variations;

(c)   the range of problems and difficulties in performing the work as seen from the point of view of those directly involved;

(d)   the flexibility of the system to variations in output or input, the way of coping with these variations and their frequency;

(e)   the present organisation structure and the relation between the working unit and other units in the enterprise;

(f)   the position of groups within this organisation, their relations with each other, any deviation in their roles and the roles of individuals from perceived roles;

(g)   the way replacements are made and training carried out, and the way the channels of communication function;

(h)   an analysis of the wages and incentive schemes.

This form of diagnosis, important as it is, can be based on interviewing, observation and the examination of various records.   It is, however, far from being an easy task, since it can raise anxieties at a time when the participants need to be reassured that modifications of current practice will turn out for the better.   It therefore needs as much tact as skill.   No attempt should be made to criticise the present system a priori or to pass judgement on the improvements needed. Besides, for the interviews to be objective, members of the working group must have confidence in the interviewer.

To illustrate this first step one may mention briefly the analysis made by the German corporation Siemens of the operations at its plant at Bad Neustadt an der Saale.[14]   This plant employs 1,800 people, of whom 400 are engaged in the production of household electrical equipment.   The company decided to focus on the operation of assembling vacuum cleaners and electric beaters.   The analysis showed that the operation consisted in:

- assembling motors for floor units;

- assembling blowers for the vacuum cleaners;

- finally assembling cleaners;

- finally assembling electric beaters.

The output and input of this production system was found to be as shown in table 1.

Table 1:   An input-output analysis at Siemens

	Motors for floor units	Blowers for cleaners	Vacuum cleaners	Electric beaters
No. of models	1	5	50	4
Production by model/month	4 000	2 000-20 000	500-20 000	4 000
No. of component parts	25	30	60	65

Quality variations were within reason.   Production was organised on assembly lines with anything between 8 and 15 workers working on each line.   The work was rather monotonous with little variety, and workers working at the different posts received short specialised training each in his particular function.   There was a wide range of models and changes in model design were frequent.   Fluctuations in demand, particularly seasonal fluctuations, presented several problems owing to the inflexibility of the system.   A survey was carried out by interviewing some 80 workers, each interview lasting approximately two hours;   the interviews were carried out by professional behavioural scientists.   The survey revealed the weaknesses of the production system and attitudinal aspects characteristic of line operators.

This type of analysis gives an over-all view of the work organisation as it exists in that plant.   It might be tempting at this stage to go into traditional consultation, say by examining the reasons for model variation, proposing a rearranged layout, etc. but it is precisely here that the present approach to work reorganisation differs, since this would contradict the two basic notions mentioned earlier, namely that operational and social problems should be examined together and that the improved method should be devised mainly by the people involved in performing the job and not by an outside agent.

Step 2: Planning the intervention

This is the second logical step and comprises the following series of activities:

(a) Decide on what is to be achieved. This has to be done in a realistic manner. On the operational side, it may be easier to define. For example, in the above case of the Siemens Company, we could set as attainable targets, the issues of greater flexibility in the production system, including the substitutability of workers, to account for changes of models and an improvement in the ergonomics situation. In other cases we could set up other targets such as the improvement of quality, the reduction of waste and the avoidance of delays. Less evident, however, is the decision on behaviourally desired targets. Thorsrud[15] defines these as follows. He also discusses them in greater detail in another chapter of this book:

- the need for a job content in the new organisation that does not demand so much in endurance but that provides variety and a certain area of decision making;

- the redesigned job that would provide an opportunity for learning;

- the redesigned job that provides a minimal degree of social support and recognition in the workplace;

- the redesigned job that leads to some sort of desirable future yet is not necessarily a promotion.

This list of socially desired targets may not be totally realistic for all situations and all people. However, it is something to strive for and to plan for. As the process of change proceeds, one may have to lower one's expectations slightly with respect to one or other of these objectives.

(b) Decide on who is to be involved and when. First, it is obvious that the people whose work is under study are to be involved in the reorganisation of their work. This includes the supervisory level. Second, staff representatives must be kept fully in the picture, from the outset about the purpose of the reorganisation, since their support is crucial. Furthermore, the timing and degree of their involvement in the reorganisation itself are matters that need to be discussed and agreed upon. Third, there are people higher up in the hierarchy whose support is needed. These should be involved from the outset in an induction seminar and kept informed of progress periodically, say every three or six months. Fourth, there are the staff and service specialists who come in contact with the working group occasionally. These may be quality control, maintenance, or other specialists. Since the redesign of work that is being attempted has to take into consideration all the activities needed for the job and not only those performed by direct workers, these specialists need to be called upon whenever the design involves a redistribution of duties or responsibilities between them and the workers directly involved or the implications of such reorganisation for other units or departments has to be examined. For example, in the Siemens case quoted earlier, any variations in the input of the production system will have implications for other departments providing component parts, while any resulting variations in the output of the finished products or proposals to reduce model changes will need to be discussed and agreed upon with the marketing department. Fifth, there is the control group. By this we mean another group performing the same function, which will act as a silent partner and a point of reference for assessing results while the reorganisations is being carried through. In most cases, and to avoid a bias in assessing results, control groups are left to work normally without being made aware of their role. More often than not, it is impossible for various reasons to use control groups and their involvement should not be considered indispensable since results can often be assessed by making comparisons with past performance.

Last, but not least, is the issue of the change agent. A change agent is a person (or a group of persons) whose task is to facilitate the introduction of the planned change in the organisation. The change agent may come from inside or outside the organisation and he performs his function by providing advisory services if and when needed. The choice of an insider versus an outsider depends on the complexity of the reorganisation needed, and the availability of qualified and acceptable people inside the organisation who can act in this capacity. A change agent has to be involved in the work from the start. He may participate in the

induction seminars, as a resource person, and in the
diagnosis phase and continues to be available for
consultation during the development of the new job
redesign and until the new organisation has stabilised, after which his role is terminated.[16] There
is, however, a very special feature relating to the
change agent in the introduction of new forms of
work organisation.   It may be useful to underline
this once more.   His task is to act as a catalyst
or at best as an agent provocateur and not as an
enlightened consultant who is setting about to
improve methods of work.   The centre of gravity in
deciding how to reorganise work and at what pace
remains with the workers directly involved.   This
very important rule governing the relation between
the change agent and the people involved should be
made clear from the very beginning and before the
work starts.

(c)   Develop the participative effort.   The essence of
new forms of work organisation is participation by
the people involved in redesigning their own work
to achieve operational, behavioural or social
objectives.   Participation is essential for at
least three compelling reasons.   In the first
instance it permits the mobilisation of as many
ideas as possible for the solution of a given problem.   Second, it gives people the chance to express
an opinion or exert an influence on a matter that is
of direct concern to them.   Third, it creates a
sense of belonging and fosters team spirit, and it
is team work that is needed in work organisation.

Participation, however, has been presented in many
cases in the literature as a cure-all.   The fact
is that it is a culture-sensitive concept and has
to relate to given situations.[17]

Successful participation patterns cannot be automatically transplanted to other situations.   Adjustments are needed for varying cultures, varying attitudes and the personalities of the people involved,
including those at the supervisory level.   The
adjustment need not mean that the participative
mechanism should be weakened to suit an authorita-
tive type of supervision.   On the contrary, attitudes may need to be influenced through seminars on
organisational development or other subjects to
accommodate participative practices.   This was the
course of action adopted in the early days of
experiences with new forms of work organisation in
Norway with respect to supervisory and managerial
staff in certain organisations.   The need for such

a course of action has to be considered as well during the planning phase of the reorganisation.

The Swedish Employers' Confederation, basing itself on conclusions from 500 shop-floor projects in Sweden,[18] has listed a number of factors that have contributed to effective participation and others that have led to poor results in Sweden. Among the latter may be cited cases where the participative programme was launched in an ambitious way, described in impressive detail possibly by a central body, a staff department or an outside consulting firm. It thus became like another company instruction. There were cases where the programme consisted mainly of endless discussions in the conference room that degenerated into petty complaints or where the whole scheme was applied in a relatively short period of time without adequate preparation. Swedish companies whose participation schemes work are those that have launched the programme with a low profile and made it simple so that the formal rules for participation are kept to a bare minimum and the objectives of participation are tangible, for example the development of new working arrangements in which discussions can concentrate on production problems and the employees' own preferences for improving themselves and their situation.

Step 3: Forming the working groups

As indicated earlier, several persons are usually involved at different times in the introduction of new forms of work organisation. This participative effort takes form through group work. Different approaches are used for different organisations and different situations. Herbst[19] identifies four approaches leading to the formation of the "work team" or "semi-autonomous group", the driving force in introducing change (see figure 2). These are:

(a) The bottom-up approach; in this the group is formed by workers on the shop floor with responsibility for a given task. The support of top management and unions is secured and the foreman is not normally included in the group. Changes at the bottom in this case can result in corresponding changes at the middle-management level.

(b) The top-down approach: this has been used by the Shell UK refineries since 1965. It consists in starting at the top to agree on a policy and continuing at successive levels of the hierarchy with a series of conferences in the expectation that this wide involvement may lead to the formation of several projects in job redesign.

Figure 2 Various approaches to forming a work team or a semi-autonomous group

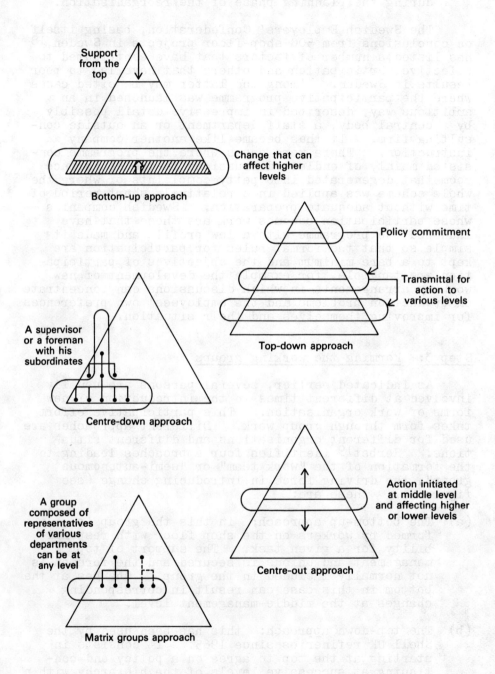

Support from the top

Change that can affect higher levels

Bottom-up approach

Policy commitment

Transmittal for action to various levels

Top-down approach

A supervisor or a foreman with his subordinates

Centre-down approach

A group composed of representatives of various departments can be at any level

Matrix groups approach

Action initiated at middle level and affecting higher or lower levels

Centre-out approach

(c)   The centre-down approach; this approach is becoming
      more and more favoured since it avoids the exclusion
      of middle management, who should have a direct
      interest in the design of new forms of organisation.
      The "work team" or the "semi-autonomous group", in
      this case, consists of workers involved in perform-
      ing the particular task with their foreman.

(d)   The centre-out approach; this is suitable for
      particular situations such as ships where the basic
      tasks are carried out by junior officers, who are
      then considered the most suitable work team.

A fifth possibility is a matrix organisation composed of persons from various departments such as specialists and non-specialists;[*] for example, in the ship
situation a work team may be formed of navigational
junior officers and junior engineers with a view to finding out whether skills can be made to overlap more
between both groups say by extending navigational training to engineers and developing some engineering skills
among navigational officers.

As a general rule and ideally this core "work team"
should not exceed six people. An increase in size to
ten or slightly more can be contemplated if the section
is well delineated and people have strong social relations. Alternatively, in a large unit, workers can be
asked to select an appropriate number to form the design
team. In other cases, where the work to be organised
calls for the use of other specialised functions, the
group may be enlarged to include production engineers,
industrial designers, cost estimators, etc. A simple
work team is found in many situations (see for example
the Matfors report).[20] The enlarged team is used to
solve more complex problems, such as product design,
production planning or materials handling problems, as
in the Saab-Scania Swedish firm, where it was called a
"development team".[21]

Whatever the composition of the team, if the experiments are being carried out in other parts of the company it is sometimes beneficial to create a so-called
"reference group", which is a central group whose task
is to guide the different working teams in their work and
keep an eye on the work being carried out in different
places. A reference group may thus be composed of
representatives of the various functions involved, plus

---

[*] See the matrix organisation discussed by Thorsrud
in Chapter 1 of this book.

a union representative, and it may be headed by a plant superintendent or the office manager, if the work is being carried out in the office, and so on.

It often happens that a project is set up for a specific purpose, say the erection of a new plant, the expansion of existing facilities, the introduction of a new product, etc. In this case a "project group" may be created, to be dissolved when the project ends. An example of project groups is the one created prior to the erection of the Volvo plant at Kalmar to make proposals for the design of the new plant which was composed of industrial engineers, supervisors and union representatives.[22] Another example is the project group created for the new pet food plant of General Foods prior to its erection at Topeka, Kansas, in the United States.[23] This project group was entrusted with the study of plant design, management philosophy, information systems, work organisation, staffing and team work at the new plant. Project groups often include workers with practical experience, who can have much to contribute. Figure 3 gives an idea of the various groups that can be involved in developing new forms of work organisation.

Perhaps the most important rule to be kept in mind is to avoid having a maze of various groups and teams with various overlapping objectives that get into each other's way or having the members of these groups frighteningly numerous. Each group should contain only those persons who are absolutely essential. In brief, common sense should dictate the type and the composition of groups that need to be established. Above all, one should keep them simple and manageable.

Step 4: Putting the groups to work

At the outset, some ground rules need to be established for the reference group, the project group or the development group. These need not be an elaborate set of detailed procedures to be followed. They would simply indicate the work to be done and an action plan for implementation. The group would define its advisory and supervisory functions, if any, and agree on the frequency and approximate duration of its meetings. As an example, in discussing procedures, a project or a reference group might decide to set up a number of subcommittees to work on different facets of a given project or to supervise the work being carried out in certain departments. The work would then be agreed upon and the composition and role of these subcommittees would become known to everybody.

Figure 3   Examples of working groups in organisations

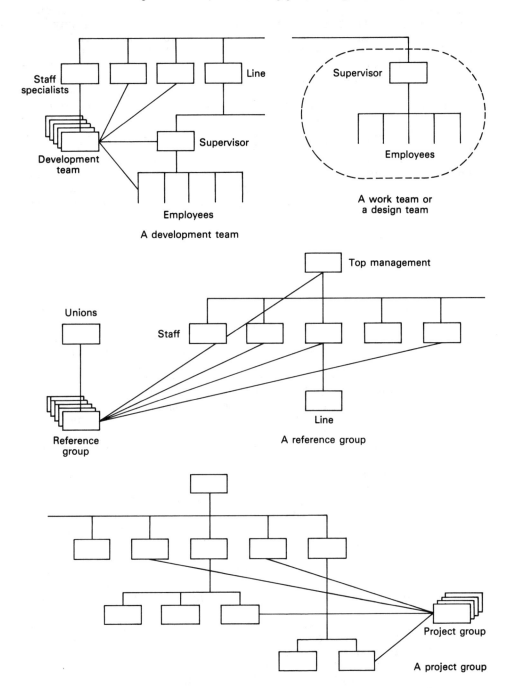

A development team

A work team or
a design team

A reference group

A project group

Two major difficulties are often encountered with reference groups, project groups and development groups. The first is that if participation has not been a way of life in the particular enterprise, members may find it difficult to get started. Progress, therefore, may be slow at the beginning. It does, however, pick up momentum as participants gradually discover that they have really a lot to contribute. The second difficulty stems from the fact that these groups are usually heterogeneous, the participants having different backgrounds and varying levels of education and experience. Industrial engineers may show little patience with detailed cost estimates and workers may feel that their appreciable experience is being overlooked in favour of some complicated model that they do not understand. Gradually, however, and given time and good group leadership, this difficulty can subside.

Putting a "work team" or a "design team" to work requires adequate preparation. This usually takes the form of a workshop lasting from one to three days. The workshop usually deals with:

(a)   an introduction to the subject of new forms of work organisation, explaining the objectives and the effect on operational and social needs. In this respect, the use of audio-visual aids is highly recommended. This introduction, usually made by the change agent, is sometimes preceded by some appropriate comments from either the line manager concerned or a senior member of the reference group or works council (if it exists). It would be an advantage to supplement it with a brief exposé from a member of another work team, in the same organisation or in another organisation, who has had experience of this work and could briefly outline how the results of his team's work were achieved. At this point, adequate time should be allowed for questions and discussions. This approach, if it can be arranged, is quite effective, for working people tend to learn more readily from each other than from outside agents. Furthermore this relation can be reinforced continuously during the project implementation phase by having groups from various enterprises exchange results and discuss problems;

(b)   methods of analysis; here the team is given some tools to enable members to analyse both the operational and personnel/social dimensions of the work. On the operational side, members are encouraged to sketch an operations process chart indicating the flow of work through the unit or section. This allows them to visualise the operation more easily and make sure that no activities have been left out. An example of such a flow is given in figure 4.

Figure 4 An example of an operation process chart (unit making zippers)

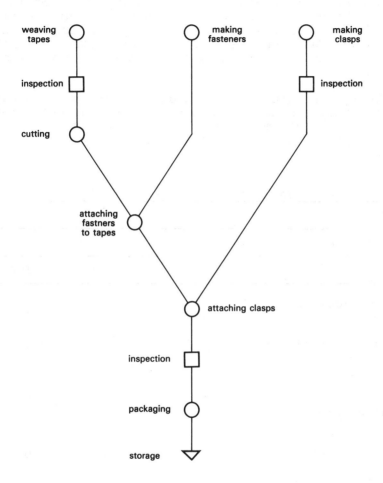

Drawing out a layout of the workplace can also enable the group to visualise clearly the position of machines, tools, equipment, storage areas, aisles and partitions, etc. This layout, which should be drawn to scale, gives the group the opportunity of evaluating the effect of any job redesign on the existing layout. Similarly, the process chart assists the group in coming to certain preliminary conclusions such as the possibility of eliminating or combining certain operations, of simplifying procedures or of modifying the job content. A further step of analysis on the operational side is the examination of the variances that occur during the performance of the job between desirable standards and the

actual.   A list of these variances or deviations from
standards may be prepared by the supervisor or an adequate staff function.   This should include deviations
from quantity and quality standards for various steps of
the operation.   A careful analysis of each variance can
lead the group to certain clues.   A further step is to
analyse the relation between the working group and other
staff functions such as quality control, planning and
maintenance functions, and to consider whether the group
can take on additional functions that would give it more
autonomy.

On the personnel/social side, the group is encouraged to examine some of the psychological aspects that
could make the job more satisfying.   The example of this
analysis given in table 2 is based on Emery and
Thorsrud.[24]

Table 2:   Work analysis, the psychological criteria

Psychological criteria	Activity			
	Job 1	Job 2	Job 3	Job 4
Scope of decision making	3	1	6	8
Degree of variety	4	3	4	6
Opportunity to learn	2	2	5	7
Mutual support and respect	2	1	0	1
Meaningful job	4	1	5	6
Desirable future	3	1	3	8

Using this table, the work team attempts to rate
each criterion on a scale, say from zero to 10 (10 being
the highest possible) for each activity (an activity
being the work performed by an individual, say a typist,
a receptionist, etc.).

In the course of examining ways of making a certain
job more satisfying, the group often hits on the idea of
job rotation or job enrichment.   A skill table, such as
table 3 allows the group to identify the required training needs and assists them in creating flexibility within

their working unit to deal with absenteeism or for
other reasons.

Table 3: Skill table

Members of the group	Skills required for the job				
	Skill 1	Skill 2	Skill 3	Skill 4	Skill 5
Employee 1	x	x		x	x
Employee 2		x	x		x
Employee 3	x	x	x		
Employee 4		x			
Employee 5		x			
Employee 6	x	x	x		

In the example of table 3 it is noticed that skill
No. 4 can be performed by only one individual
(employee 1).   Similarly, employees 4 and 5 are unable
to replace any others if variety is to be introduced in
the job or in case of an emergency.   This table therefore points out ·the desired training needs if group work
is to be introduced.

By providing such simple tools, the workshop will
have served a useful purpose.   The rest is left to the
group.   The role of the resource person or change agent
is to be close at hand in case of need but not to interfere directly.   This is necessary if we want to create
in the group a capacity to think for itself and to innovate without developing a dependence on outside help all
the time.   The work of the team, then, can continue
through regular meetings of possibly an hour a week or
so.

Step 5: Evaluating continuously and
        confronting problems early

Several problems arise during the implementation of
new forms of work organisation.   It is usually possible
to anticipate some of them.   As an example, there may be
problems related to a changing role of the supervisor or
to redundancy, brought about by changing the role of
certain specialists, say, quality controllers or product

inspectors, should the team decide to take on these functions. There may be problems related to the synchronisation of work if the group changes its output or to the need for further training by certain members or for technical consultation with specialists inside or outside the organisation (say on a more suitable materials-handling system).

These are natural developments, many of which could have been foreseen. Both management and the unions (and for that matter the reference group) should expect problems, particularly at the early stages, and they have to be prepared to devote some energy to solving them. Failure to confront these problems early can create frustration and a feeling that "the project has failed".

It is impossible to give a list of all the problems that can arise during implementation in all types of situations. Some of the commonest problems, however, often concern the earlier attempts at job redesign by the team. The proposed design may lean more towards individual job enrichment than group work or may leave several questions unanswered. Groups may be timid in suggesting changes of supervision practices or social relations because of inherent cultural barriers and so on. A change agent can carefully suggest to the group the re-examination of its proposal in the light of what was outlined in the introductory workshop. Problems related to retraining need not be difficult to handle if the training unit in the organisation is given adequate notice.

Problems of synchronising a changing team's output with that of preceding and subsequent units are problems that used to be discussed at the reference group level. Several approaches to deal with it have been suggested in the chapter on the design of production systems (for example, the establishment of buffer stock).

More sensitive problems are those related to possible redundancy, the changing role of supervision and of specialists and sharing the benefits of increased productivity if any. These have to be faced case by case in a joint effort by management and unions, sometimes through bargaining to reach a mutually acceptable solution. Some companies, like ICI (UK), have in fact resorted to concluding a collective agreement on productivity sharing prior to work reorganisation.[25]

Step 6: Assessing results

It can happen that the measurement of results is
expressed in very vague terms, "the working climate has
greatly improved", or that only some dimensions are
measured in reasonable detail, others being overlooked
or treated superficially. This is comprehensible. In
the first instance, some of the consequences of work
organisation are inter-related, whereas others are only
partly so. For example, it may be easier to claim that
quality has improved as a result. It is more difficult,
however, to claim that this has resulted in expanded
sales. The latter result may be due to other factors
besides improved quality. Assessment work is an intri-
cate task and the choice of evaluation criteria depends
on the purpose. If it is needed for research purposes
then refined questionnaires may be developed to measure
attitudinal changes or to give an indication of job
satisfaction. Most managers, however, are more interested in simple tangible criteria such as productivity,
absenteeism, quality, waste and general attitude to work.
Nor should one overlook that improvements in work organisation are generally achieved at a certain cost. There
may be expense resulting from rearranging layout or from
investment in new materials-handling equipment or from
higher wages. Thus, the first step in the evaluation
exercise consists in setting up a list of operational
benefits and costs. Table 4 gives an indication of some
of the most important criteria that could be taken into
consideration in evaluating tangible operational results.

More difficult, however, is the assessment of
increased or decreased satisfaction with the job or of
behavioural and attitudinal changes. Some of the indicators used for job satisfaction are essentially those
used earlier in table 2, namely:

- Whether the new job redesign allows the group a
  greater freedom of planning and decision making.

- Whether there is sufficient variety.

- The opportunity to learn and to go on learning on
  the job.

- Whether there is mutual support between the team
  and other working groups or departments.

- Whether the job is socially meaningful.

- Whether it can lead to some sort of desirable
  future.

Table 4: Some operational cost and benefit criteria

Possible benefits

- Higher productivity, measured as value-added or as
  the ratio of output to man-hours worked or output
  to materials used; the measurement indicator used
  will depend on the particular situation at the workplace.

- Less waste of material, assessed by estimating the
  cost of scrap and rejects before and after the work
  reorganisation.

- Higher quality, in many cases measured in terms of
  frequency of variation from quality control limits;
  and also as the cost of reworking rejects.

- Lower carrying costs computed for inventories.

- Less variety in materials and components, resulting
  in shorter time of operations, could also be reflected in the productivity measurement index.

- Lower maintenance costs that may result if workers
  take direct responsibility for routine maintenance
  operations.

- Reduced costs of other staff activities, such as
  quality control, if the group assumes responsibility
  for them.

- Reduced costs of turnover and absenteeism, a factor
  that needs to be measured over an extended period.
  This cost is derived in an estimated manner since
  it can vary from one occupation to another.

- Reduced cost of supervision that may result if the
  group reorganises work in such a way that the role
  of the supervisory staff is modified or curtailed.

Possible costs

- Cost of buying additional machinery, tools or equipment, particularly such things as materials-handling
  equipment, containers or racks for buffer stock.
  This cost needs to be calculated in terms of annual
  depreciation value.

- Cost of changing the layout, including cost of
  additional space, if any, or of moving various
  machines or equipment.

194

Table 4 (concl.)

- Cost of improving the physical working environment
  to make it safer and to improve working conditions.

- Carrying cost for additional buffer stock if this
  has to be increased to introduce flexibility at the
  work stations.

- Higher training cost as a result of the multi-
  skilling that may be needed for the members of the
  various work teams.

- Possible increased cost resulting from a new wage
  and incentive scheme, say by moving from individual
  incentives to group incentives.

In 1967 Shell UK used a questionnaire to be completed by department managers, which aimed at detecting
whether changes had occurred over the preceding year in
the following areas related to job satisfaction:[10]

- variety of tasks;

- job targets and knowledge of results;

- learning on the job;

- increased areas for decision making;

- increased participation in problem solving;

- support and recognition;

- relation of job to company or community;

- desirable future;

- signs of increased responsibility and commitment to
  a change of attitudes.

Other enterprises, using a variation of the above-
mentioned criteria, resorted to detailed interviews and
more sophisticated measures of attitudinal change.
Interviews and questionnaires (open-ended and/or structured), before and after the change, designed to assess
increased job satisfaction and/or attitudinal change, are
the commonest tools used; yet for an amateur or even an
inexperienced professional, it is easy to introduce a
bias inadvertently in any of the questions. Even if the
tool used is considered adequate, it is possible that
some participants may score lower on a job satisfaction

questionnaire, after the changes have been introduced in the job, despite the apparent greater involvement and attachment to the newer method of work. This could happen as a result of an increased awareness of work problems through the various stages of implementation.[26]

Finally, one should mention that some enterprises prefer to think of work organisation as an ongoing process and try to avoid the notion of "final solutions" on the occasion of which a proper detailed assessment of results is made. They therefore prefer to assess only certain major criteria at given points in time, say, once every six months or every year.

3. Enhancing the chances of success

In outlining the method by which new forms of work organisation can be introduced, several points were raised at each step, indicating what need or need not be done. Over-all, however, there are certain factors, the observance of which can enhance substantially the chances of success. Foremost among these factors is the existence of a sound and healthy industrial relations environment. One can only court failure if major labour management relations problems are looming in the background. At all times every effort must be made to secure the conviction and commitment of both the working group and those at various levels of management and in trade unions who while not being directly involved can influence the progress of the work being done. To this end, as many workshops as may be necessary should be carried out within the enterprise at various phases of the project's initiation and implementation. Needless to say, this process of securing support can readily fail if there are frequent changes in the personnel involved. Every effort must be made, therefore, to ascertain the relative stability of the persons associated with the work reorganisation project over its lifetime.

The choice of a worksite and/or a problem area that is a candidate for work reorganisation must be done with care, particularly at the early stages in an enterprise. The problem to be examined must be both meaningful and manageable. It should present an interesting and stimulating exercise with a learning experience and should tackle both the technical aspect of performing the job as well as its behavioural and social aspects. Examples of the latter would be issues of job enrichment and better working conditions. The problem must also be manageable in the sense that its dimensions should match the group's ability to solve it, and the proposed solutions and their ramifications present a realistic and a cost-effective course of action.   Success will also be more readily achieved if the work group feel that they are the real originators and implementors of the desired change, that it is neither the brainchild of an outside consultant nor management, in other words, if they internalise the problem.   That is why it has been stressed earlier in this chapter that a change agent must adhere strictly to his role as a facilitator and a catalyst, and avoid providing direct instructions or volunteering solutions.   This secures group commitment to the proposed change more easily.   Equally important, however, is the fact that a work group can derive as much satisfaction from the whole process of initiating and introducing a new working arrangement as it does from the end result, and as such the whole exercise must be seen as theirs and the ideas as emanating from the group members.

One of the most important factors that needs to be taken into consideration from the outset is the issue of wages and incentives.   Through work redesign, the job content can and may change, workers may acquire new skills or added responsibility.   This calls for a new evaluation of the changed jobs with a corresponding modification of the wages structure.   Similarly, group work implies a shift from individual incentives to group incentives.   By reconsidering wages and incentives, management demonstrates that the organisation rewards people for positive end results, which is only fair.

Finally, through new forms of work organisation, change can become institutionalised within an organisation, stimulating creativity and rejuvenating the organisation as it spreads from one problem area to another. As such, it should not be looked upon as an isolated experiment but as an ongoing process and as a viable and effective approach to problem solving.

4.   How they did it

Case 1 - A Swedish glassware company[27]

The AB Orrefors Glasbruck Company consists of four manufacturing units.   The largest is located at Orrefors and employs 300 people.

The art glass industry as a whole has been suffering from a gradual deterioration in profitablity.   The problems faced by the production departments were summarised as follows:

(1) slow production flow, due to long production pro-
     cesses;

(2) inflexible organisation, every operation (say rough-
     ing or smoothing) being considered specialised and
     being performed by one or few workers;

(3) a very high rate of rejects;

(4) a rather awkward wage system based on piecework,
     which made it difficult to move people from one job
     to another;

(5) many monotonous jobs in the finishing department.

The company contacted a consulting firm. The firm
proposed shifting from piece-work to daily rates based
on well established norms of production and detailed
planning by supervisors of employees' work on an hour-by-
hour basis. The enforcement of this course of action
would have entailed a substantial increase in the number
of supervisors.

After some hesitation, the management decided to
go in the opposite direction, that is, to seek a solution
that would continue the traditional relations it has
always enjoyed with its workers by shifting a substantial
amount of control and supervision to the workers themselves.

In 1969, the management decided to initiate experiments in new forms of work organisation and sounded out
the employees, who manifested an interest in co-operating.
The Swedish Employers' Organisation was requested to
assist as a change agent. A reference group was
formed of representatives of employees, the supervisors,
the production engineers and management to supervise the
experiments. The reference group set three basic objectives: higher productivity, more job satisfaction and
greater security. Members of the group read various
books, reports and articles on the subject and visited
three other companies where similar work was done. The
group decided to tackle work organisation first and then
examine the wages system. The actual redesign of the
work was left to the people involved, workers and designers with assistance from methods people and designers.
It was decided to start the work at the edge-grinding
department.

The design team then set to work. An analysis of
the situation showed that the layout was of the functional type, that is, all machines that had a similar
function were grouped together. The team decided to
experiment with a flow layout by rearranging the layout in

such a way that the machines were arranged in individual product lines.   The very varied nature of the product range made it impossible to change to flow layout altogether.

After some thinking, it was decided to divide the product range into several groups and arrange the production equipment sections with each section capable of producing the relevant product variety.   To complete this approach, several other measures were introduced; it was decided that each working group would correct its own faults so that only finished products would leave the section.   Another measure was to encourage workers to broaden their range of skills by attempting to master as many tasks as possible within the group and so to create the flexibility needed.   The result of all this was a substantial increase in volume with a smaller in-process inventory.   The quality also improved.

Next, it was decided to tackle the wages system. At an early stage it was agreed that a check on productivity needed to be kept.   A productivity index was established to measure output in relation to the number of hours put in by the group.   Since the output was quite varied, the index was readjusted several times to reach a more equitable measure.   It was then agreed that the wages would consist of an individual monthly wage, plus a production premium that would be paid only when a certain productivity level was surpassed.   Furthermore, when a decision had to be made on the method of payment of the production premium, it was easy to make.   Since each individual's work had become varied, it was agreed that the premium would be linked to the group's joint results.

The following step consisted in spreading the experimentation to various other departments.   This was done with considerable success.   The company then set up certain evaluation criteria in terms of productivity, rejects and wages development compared with the industry as a whole and they all indicated favourable results. Five years later a simple attitude survey was carried out using personal interviews.   The results showed a favourable attitude with respect to the new organisation.

Case 2 - An Indian post office[28]

Influenced by ideas on work reorganisation given in a postal training seminar, two of the participants (training officers) together with the Director of Postal Training became interested in applying these principles to a postal office in the city of Simla, the native town of one of the training officers.   After visiting all the post offices in the city, studying the work flow and the work environment and interviewing employees at random, they decided to start at the Chaura Maidan post office in Simla, which had 43 employees and one part-timer. Among these, two were union leaders. Some of the active employees, including the sub-postmaster, who was in charge of that post office, were involved in a preliminary diagnostic study, which showed that:

- the working space in the office was inadequate and congested, with abundant antiquated and dysfunctional furniture and old records;

- the lighting was poor;

- there was no physical facility at the counters for customers who had to fill in forms or sitting accommodation for the old and infirm.

Action was therefore immediately initiated to remedy these defects. More space was created, functional furniture was brought in, the old stock of records was disposed of and a recreation room for the staff was created. Simultaneously, a more careful analysis of the work system was carried out by the employees, who were encouraged to come forward and work with the change agents. The analysis showed that the activities of the post office consisted of:

(a) Mail delivery activities: collection and delivery of mail, including accountable items such as registered letters, money orders, etc.

(b) Counter service activities: these included savings bank function, booking of money orders, registration of letters and parcels, selling of postage stamps and postal orders, registration of broadcast receiving licences, etc. Each function was performed at one specialised counter. Thus the registration was done at one counter, while postage stamps selling was carried out at another, and so on.

(c) Cable and telephone activities: receipt and despatch of telegrams, settlement of telephone bills and maintenance of the telephone booth.

(d) Control functions, including treasury activities: supervisory activities, maintenance of records and correspondence with other offices, including superior authorities.

The counter activities were carried out by employees specialising in one of the functions and the whole office seemed to follow the same pattern. Sorting postmen carried out sorting activities, delivery postmen did the detailed sorting and delivery, delivery clerks maintained records of accountable items and so on.

Following this diagnosis, a series of meetings was held with the employees and the change agent in search of a better system that would relieve them from undue pressure of work and at the same time render a better service to the clients. Gradually, a delivery group was created, which included the sorting postmen, the delivery postmen, the clerks concerned with the maintenance of records and the assistant postmaster. The work layout was redesigned and the group decided to reallocate work itself. Gradually the system became stabilised, with the result that the sorting and delivery of mail were cut down by about three-quarters of an hour per shift. The problem of absenteeism was easier to handle since the group now found it easier to redistribute work in a more equitable way.

Next, the problem of the counter system was tackled. Through proper training it was found that it was more advantageous to conduct all the various activities at each counter except for savings bank activities. This enabled the clients to transact all their business at one counter instead of running from one counter to another. As a result, pressure on the counters became equitably distributed and variety was introduced in the work itself. It was also possible for the counter clerks to take their lunch break in turn, closing down one counter at a time without creating particular problems. Even the telegraph signallers were integrated with the group, since, whenever they had free time, they could volunteer to lend a helping hand to the delivery group. There was, however, a problem in that the role of the sub-postmaster became somewhat ambiguous and he was not sure what degree of discipline and supervision he could exercise in the new system. There were also occasional problems, but the change agents refused to interfere and the two groups were advised to sort out their own problems with the sub-postmaster.

With the reasonable success obtained, the experiment spread to two other post offices in Simla. Some employees from Chaura Maidan were encouraged to visit the two new experimental sites and offer help. The three experiments were carried out on a low key. While higher authorities of the post office, like the Postmaster General, were kept informed, the experimental sites were not exposed to the top brass during the first year of the experiment in 1975. Later on, internal publicity was given and senior officials came down and examined the new system.

It is perhaps interesting to note that transplanting the same experiences to certain post offices in Delhi proved more difficult. Thus, in some offices it was not easy at first to integrate the delivery group on account of the role and status differential between sorting postmen and delivery postmen, which did not present a significant problem at Simla. However, this problem was later overcome and it was possible to introduce the multiple counter system with some variation from the Simla system. It is also interesting to note that this multi-counter operation was introduced and accepted by the group, whereas, in the past several attempts to introduce the multiple counter system in the post offices, made through various reports and recommendations, had never reached the stage of implementation.

Case 3 - A Tanzanian handling and forwarding enterprise[5]

This enterprise, which employs 180 persons, diagnosed its problem as being the need to improve the maintenance operation of its fleet of trucks. After attending an induction workshop organised by the ILO in Dar es Salaam, management endorsed the idea of choosing the maintenance workshop as a worksite and pledged its full support. Analysis of the work situation at the workshop showed that four major skills were performed: mechanical repairs, auto-electric wiring, panel beating and tyre repairs. Twelve people were permanently employed but only four were skilled mechanics in each of these operations. The skilled mechanics performed their work as they could fit it in, while the rest of the workers assisted as required. Because of the pressure of work on these four mechanics, the enterprise carried a good number of repairs elsewhere. At the same time the unskilled workers complained of the lack of opportunities for training and promotion. Following an internal meeting, the workshop workers decided that each of the skilled mechanics would train three other workers in his speciality. This was carried out and then each group of trainees was shifted for similar training by each of the other mechanics, so that within a year each of the workers had become reasonably skilled in the various maintenance jobs at the workshop. Testing showed that all but one had acquired a good grasp of all the operations involved. The company management encouraged those who were willing to attend evening courses at the local vocational training school and financed their participation. Two did so and passed the skilled trade test. The work group then decided to rotate in performing their tasks. The net result was that outside maintenance work became unnecessary, a more co-operative spirit ensued and there were increased opportunities for learning. The wages of workers were then revised to correspond to the newly acquired and upgraded skills.

Management then decided to encourage the introduction of new forms of work organisation at the packing and carpentry section. Packers and carpenters worked almost separate from each other. The packers made estimates of the packing space required. The carpenters then manufactured the containers, which were later used by the packers. A joint work group was formed which decided on a combined operation, packers were shown how to assist with some elementary carpentry and carpenters were taught how to pack. In cases where packers were away for estimating jobs, carpenters helped with the final packing; similarly packers assisted carpenters if need be in manufacturing containers. As a result, productivity improved and the company began to receive a good number of letters praising its services. Both jobs were upgraded and wages were increased.

This success prompted the company to turn its attention to the heavy-lift section. Representatives of the working group undertook the function of planning and distributing the work assignments of that section and introduced the necessary training to enable more flexible working arrangements. They also examined the working conditions at the section and undertook several measures. Management, on its side, invited the workers' views when acquiring new trucks and heavy-lifting equipment. They also advised on the acquisition of spare parts. Within two years, the rate of utilisation of vehicles and equipment increased substantially. The common practice of leasing cranes.elsewhere became a rare event, as workers found that with better planning it was possible to rely solely on the enterprise's own cranes. Similarly, a markedly improved safety record was obtained and the rate of absenteeism was halved in two years. Wages were then revised upwards in line with the enlarged job content and the newly acquired skills.

5. A concluding remark

The introduction of new forms of work organisation is a challenging process that requires adequate preparation, participation and support by all concerned. An attempt has been made to outline the various factors that need to be considered and to give a guide for implementation. This step-by-step approach, which sounds like a highly structured guideline, is intended to act as a reminder that certain stages and points should not be overlooked. What can vary from one situation to another is the way in which each step is to be performed, and this can be dictated only by common sense.

Perhaps the greatest value of work reorganisation is one that eludes measurement, the ability to create within the organisation centres for change, which attempt to reconcile operational objectives continuously with needs satisfaction.

6. References

[1] Lindholm, Rolf, and Norstedt, Jan-Peder: The Volvo report (Stockholm, Swedish Employers' Confederation, 1975).

[2] Johansen Ragnar: Changes in work planning increase shipboard democracy: The first 3 years of experience from M/S Balao (Oslo, Work Research Institute, 1976).

[3] Kanawaty, George and Thorsrud, Einar: "Field experiences in new forms of work organisation", in International Labour Review, International Labour Office, Geneva, May-June 1981.

[4] Carby, Keith: Job redesign in practice (London, Institute of Personnel Management, 1976).

[5] Kanawaty, George: "Managers' concerns in the next decade: Social systems and human welfare in organisations", in Human Futures (New Delhi), Vol. 2, No. 1, 1979.

[6] Maynard, H.B.: Production, an international appraisal of contemporary manufacturing systems and the changing role of the worker (London, McGraw-Hill, 1975).

[7] Beckhard, R.: Organisation development: Strategies and models (Reading, Massachusetts, Addison-Wesley, 1969).

[8] Greiner, L.: "Patterns of organisation change", in Harvard Business Review, Vol. 45, No. 3, 1967.

[9] Schein, Edgar H.: Process consultation: Its role in organisational development (Reading, Massachusetts, Addison-Wesley, 1969).

[10] Hill, Paul: Towards a new philosophy of management, the company development programme of Shell U.K. Limited (London, Gower Press, 1971).

[11] Hackman, J.: "Work design", in J. Hackman and J. Suttle (eds.): Improving life at work, behavioural science approaches to organisational change (Santa Monica, California, Goodyear Publishing Co., 1977).

[12] Marchington, M.P.: "Worker participation and plant-wide incentive systems", in Personnel Review, Vol. 6, No. 3, 1977.

[13] Whitsett, David: "Where are your unenriched jobs?", in Harvard Business Review, Vol. 53, No. 1, Jan.-Feb. 1975.

[14] International Labour Office, New Forms of Work Organisation, Vol. 1, Geneva, 1979.

[15] Thorsrud, Einar: "Policy-making as a learning process, a worknote on social science policy", in A.B. Cherns: Social Science and Government Policies and Problems (Tavistock Publications Ltd., 1972)

[16] Ottaway, Richard and Cooper, Cary: "Moving toward a taxonomy of change agents", in International Studies of Management and Organisation, Vol. VIII, Nos. 1-2, Spring-Summer, 1978.

[17] Strauss, George: Improving the quality of work life, managerial practices (Springfield, Va., US Department of Commerce, June 1975).

[18] Swedish Employers' Confederation: Job reform in Sweden, conclusions from 500 shop floor projects (Stockholm, 1975).

[19] Herbst, P.G.: Alternatives to hierarchies (Leiden, Martinus-Nijhoff, 1976).

[20] Törner, Pär: The Matfors report (Stockholm, Swedish Employers' Confederation, 1976).

[21] Norstedt, Jan-Peder and Agurén, Stefan: The Saab-Scania report (Stockholm, Swedish Employers' Confederation, 1973).

[22] Agurén, Stefan, Hansson, Reine and Karlsson, K.G.: The Volvo Kalmar plant, the impact of new design on work organisation (Stockholm, The Rationalisation Council, SAF/LO, 1976).

[23] Ketchum, L. (General Foods): Experience of advances in work organisation, paper submitted to the International Management Seminar on Advances in Work Organisation, Organisation for Economic Co-operation and Development, Paris, 1973.

[24] Emery, Fred and Thorsrud, Einar: Democracy at work (Leiden, Martinus-Nijhoff, 1976).

[25] Owen, Trevor (Imperial Chemical Industries Limited) in Advances in work organisation, supplement to the Final Report (Paris; Organisation for Economic Co-operation and Development, 1973).

[26] Cameran, S., Orchin, K. and White, G.C.: Improving satisfaction at work by job redesign (London), Work Research Unit Report No. 1, May 1974.

[27] Norén, Anders E. and Norstedt, Jan-Peder: The Orrefors report (Stockholm, Swedish Employers' Confederation, 1975).

[28] International Labour Office: New Forms of Work Organisation, Vol. 2 (Geneva, 1979); see also De, Nitish R.: Initiation process in designing new forms of work organisation: tentative experiences from India, unpublished paper, 1978.